Good News from Latin America

GLOBAL LIBRARY

This volume is a fitting tribute by Langham scholars from Latin America to the global and holistic vision of faith and mission championed by John Stott. Carrying forward that legacy, the authors ably contextualize the witness of the evangelical church to the realities of Latin America. They also rightly critique recent voices who doubt whether these faith communities are truly heirs of the Reformation. Biblically informed and deeply rooted in Latin American history and life, these essays offer a broad set of reflections that would delight the man they honor.

M. Daniel Carroll R. (Rodas), PhD
Scripture Press Ministries Professor of Biblical Studies and Pedagogy,
Wheaton College, Illinois, USA

The Bible is intrinsically linked to its context, a connection that extends seamlessly into the realm of theology. Embracing this contextual nature allows us to effectively communicate the core message of the good news (buenas nuevas). In turn, this aids the church in self-reflection and paves the way for wider societal transformation. This book excels in realizing these objectives. Moreover, its methodology provides a template for international adoption, hopefully signalling a leap towards a "glocal" theology that blends global perspectives with local nuances.

Riad A. Kassis, PhD
International Director, Langham Partnership International

This book provides its readers a full theological menu with food grown in Latin America, and prepared by cooks who are working or have worked in Latin America. The book is delicious! It is competent, global yet grounded in its land, irenic yet challenging of paradigms that once again attempt to colonize Latin America with a gospel that does not take into account what our Lord is doing in our continent. This is a must-read. I sincerely hope that instructors around the world will assign it in their respective courses.

Osvaldo Padilla, PhD
Professor of New Testament and Theology,
Beeson Divinity School, Samford University, Alabama, USA

Good News from Latin America

Reflections in Honor of John Stott

Edited by

Nelson R. Morales Fredes

This English edition © 2024 Langham Publishing

Original title in Spanish: *Buenas nuevas desde América Latina: Reflexiones en honor a John Stott*
© 2021 Centro de Investigaciones y Publicaciones - Ediciones Puma, Jesús María, Lima - Perú.
This translation is published by written agreement with the Research and Publications Center - Ediciones Puma

Published 2024 by Langham Global Library
An imprint of Langham Publishing
www.langhampublishing.org

Langham Publishing and its imprints are a ministry of Langham Partnership

Langham Partnership
PO Box 296, Carlisle, Cumbria, CA3 9WZ, UK
www.langham.org

ISBNs:
978-1-83973-928-6 Print
978-1-78641-017-7 ePub
978-1-78641-018-4 PDF

Nelson R. Morales Fredes hereby asserts his moral right to be identified as the Author of the General Editor's part in the Work in accordance with sections 77 and 78 of the Copyright, Designs and Patents Act 1988.

All rights reserved. No part of this publication may be reproduced, stored in a retrieval system or transmitted, in any form or by any means, electronic, mechanical, photocopying, recording or otherwise, without the prior written permission of the publisher or the Copyright Licensing Agency.

Requests to reuse content from Langham Publishing are processed through PLSclear. Please visit www.plsclear.com to complete your request.

All Scripture quotations, unless otherwise indicated, are taken from the Holy Bible, New International Version®, NIV®. Copyright ©1973, 1978, 1984, 2011 by Biblica, Inc.™ Used by permission of Zondervan.

Scripture quotations marked (NRSV) are taken from the New Revised Standard Version Bible, copyright © 1989 National Council of the Churches of Christ in the United States of America. Used by permission. All rights reserved.

Scripture quotations marked MSG are taken from *The Message*, copyright © 1993, 2002, 2018 by Eugene H. Peterson. Used by permission of NavPress. All rights reserved. Represented by Tyndale House Publishers.

British Library Cataloguing-in-Publication Data
A catalogue record for this book is available from the British Library

ISBN: 978-1-83973-928-6

Cover & Book Design: projectluz.com
Photo by Florian Delée on Unsplash

Langham Partnership actively supports theological dialogue and an author's right to publish but does not necessarily endorse the views and opinions set forth here or in works referenced within this publication, nor can we guarantee technical and grammatical correctness. Langham Partnership does not accept any responsibility or liability to persons or property as a consequence of the reading, use or interpretation of its published content.

Contents

Contributors ix

Introduction 1
    Nelson R. Morales Fredes

1 Latin America Protestant History 7
    J. Daniel Salinas

2 Images of God in Latin America 23
    Nelson R. Morales Fredes

3 The Gospel in the Haystack 33
    Sadrac Meza

4 The Bible, Female Leadership, and Latin American Hermeneutics .. 47
    Javier Ortega Badilla

5 Reading the Bible "Naturally": Loving God and Your Neighbor through a Contextual Hermeneutic (Matthew 19:1–12) 61
    Juan José Barreda Toscano

6 The Church: A School for Double Citizenship 77
    Ruth Padilla DeBorst

7 A Crisis in Latin American Evangelical Leadership: Between Intolerance and Incongruity 93
    Dinorah B. Méndez

8 Protestants, Democracy, and Citizenship 101
    Darío López Rodriguez

9 Decolonizing Christianity: Clothing Ourselves in the Gospel of the Kingdom of God 119
    Marcelo Vargas A.

10 Outline of a Latin American Socioenvironmental Theology 131
    Víctor Manuel Morales Vásquez

11 The Discernment Community as a Paradigm for a Continuing Reformation 145
    Rafael Zaracho

Contributors

Juan José Barreda Toscano, Peruvian. PhD in theology with emphasis on sacred Scriptures from Instituto Universitario ISEDET, Argentina. Director of Bíblica Virtual: Comunidad de estudios contextuales. Professor of biblical hermeneutics at Universidad del Centro Educativo Latinoamericano - UCEL.

Darío López Rodríguez, Peruvian. PhD in evangelicals and human rights from the Oxford Centre for Mission Studies, UK. Pastor of the Church of God of Peru, Lima. Professor at the Facultad Evangélica Orlando Costas.

Dinorah B. Méndez, Mexican. PhD in theology from the Oxford Centre for Mission Studies, UK. Retired professor after thirty years of teaching at the Seminario Teológico Bautista Mexicano. For the Baptist World Alliance, vice president of the Commission on Baptist Heritage & Identity (2020–2025) and member of the Commission on Theological Education.

Sadrac Meza, Costa Rican. PhD in systematic theology from Trinity International University, Illinois, USA. Professor at the Seminario ESEPA in San José, Costa Rica.

Nelson R. Morales Fredes, Chilean. PhD in theological studies with emphasis on New Testament from Trinity International University, Illinois, USA. Professor at the Seminario Teológico Centroamericano, Guatemala.

Víctor Manuel Morales Vásquez, Mexican. PhD in theology from the University of Liverpool, UK. Teacher of evangelical religion, philosophy, and Spanish in elementary and middle school at the Georg-Müller Schule, Bielefeld, Germany.

Javier Ortega Badilla, Chilean. PhD in theology with emphasis on sacred Scripture from the Instituto Universitario ISEDET, Argentina. Pastor of a Christian and Missionary Alliance church. Professor of New Testament at the Seminario Teológico Alianza and at the Evangelical Theological Community of Chile.

Ruth Padilla DeBorst, born in Colombia, raised in Argentina, and living in Costa Rica. PhD in theology, with emphasis on missiology and social ethics from Boston University, Massachusetts, USA. President of CETI Continental, member of Casa Adobe.

J. Daniel Salinas, Colombian. PhD in historical theology from Trinity International University, Illinois, USA. Professor at the Fundación Universitaria Seminario Bíblico de Colombia. Associate director of Mesa Scholar, a program of Mesa Global.

Marcelo Vargas A., Bolivian. PhD in anthropological missiology from the Oxford Centre for Mission Studies and University of Wales, UK. Teacher and director of the Centro de Capacitación Misionera in La Paz, Bolivia.

Rafael Zaracho, Paraguayan. PhD in theology from University of St. Andrews, UK. Professor at the Instituto Bíblico Asunción, Paraguay.

Introduction

Nelson R. Morales Fredes

John Stott and Latin America

During 2021 we celebrated the centennial anniversary of the birth of John Robert Walmsley Stott, better known among his close friends as "Uncle John." I learned more about him during my years of doctoral studies at Trinity International University (TIU/TEDS) in Chicago than in all my previous years. During those years, I had the privilege of hearing directly from people quite close to John about his passion for the Jesus he proclaimed. Without a doubt, the life and influence of John Stott will guide us for many more years.

Although he was born in London in 1921, he had a heart for the world from early in his life. His father sent him to Germany and France to perfect his foreign language abilities, but he did not know that he was preparing him to serve the global church. His connection with Latin America began to develop when he met "the Latin American Three Musketeers" at the Lausanne Congress in 1974: René Padilla, Samuel Escobar, and Orlando Costas. In this way, a closeness began to grow between Stott and the Majority World. As J. P. Greenman states, "continued fellowship with Christians in the developing world heightened Stott's sensitivity to issues of poverty and injustice, helping him to develop his increasingly holistic understanding of the gospel."[1]

This more holistic vision of the gospel is what motivates us to write this book. We would like to give tribute to the legacy of John Stott as academicians of the Langham Scholars program. Thanks to his vision we have been able to study, develop our talents, and serve the Lord in and from Latin America. Instead of giving biographical details, I would like to share a couple of anecdotes from influential Latin American scholars who had the privilege of a close friendship with John Stott.

An anecdote that has had a great impact in my life is one that René Padilla has frequently shared. He relates that, on one of their many trips together, he

---

1. J. P. Greenman, "Stott, John Robert Walmsley," *Biographical Dictionary of Evangelicals*, eds. Timothy Larsen, D. W. Bebbington, and Mark A. Noll (Downers Grove, IL: InterVarsity Press, 2003), 640.

went to Buenos Aires airport to pick up John Stott. It was raining cats and dogs. When they reached René's home, they left their muddy shoes in the entrance. The next morning, when René arose, he found John shining Rene's shoes. René felt a bit embarrassed and asked, "John, what are you doing?" Stott answered that the Lord taught us to wash each other's feet, but given that René's feet did not need to be washed, John wanted to serve him by shining his shoes.

Another anecdote comes from Jorge Atiencia. Jorge tells a story from when they were in Cuba. As frequently happened in those years, the electricity went off. Dirty plates began to pile up in the kitchen from the seventy participants who had gathered to hear John's biblical expositions, for, as we know, in Latin America, without electricity there is no water. At 6 a.m. the next morning, Jorge relates, "I heard a noise in the kitchen. Electricity had returned, together with the running water. Stott was washing the dirty dishes of all the participants and invited me to join him. He was a servant who served quietly."

Both stories illustrate a profound aspect of John's character that he has transmitted to us: humble servanthood. This humble service shows other characteristics of John: he considered others his equals, he learned from what they said and did, and involved them in the mutual process of learning. That describes this book project as well. We have walked together, learning from each other and enjoying the simplicity of each person's company and mutual service. Without a doubt, Stott's life and character has shaped our lives as Langham scholars.

The Context of Current Research

In 2017, the Protestant Reformation commemorated its five hundreth anniverary. Celebrations were organized almost everywhere. Congresses, symposiums, books, magazine articles, and numerous programs on the radio and on YouTube took place. We Langham Scholars found ourselves together in a working meeting in Medellín, Colombia. Among the many ideas and proposals that circulated, what caught our attention was the euphoria that some affirmations demonstrated in books published in Spanish by the movement called *Coalición por el Evangelio* (The Gospel Coalition), as will be seen later in this book.

This movement, recently arrived in Latin America but with an important power of communication, maintained that the Protestant Reformation had never reached Latin America and that it was only through their movement that the gospel was penetrating into these regions. Without a doubt, both claims were, at the very least, exaggerations. Nevertheless, it was a good moment to reflect on certain questions: When did the Reformation arrive in Latin America? What gospel are we referring to when we think of Christianity in Latin America?

To honor the contributions of John Stott, we decided to take on this project. The support of Riad Kassis, then director of the Langham Scholars Ministry, was crucial. Given that we express our responses from the Latin American context, we decided to title this book *Good News from Latin America* (*Buenas Nuevas desde América Latina*). We agreed on some basic writing guidelines, but as typically happens in this type of project, the end result did not exactly follow the original plan. With gratitude for the financial contribution of Langham Scholars and, in particular, the support of Stefanii Ferenczi Morton, we were able to hold a conference in the Seminario Teológico Centroamericano in 2019. There we presented almost all the chapters to a diverse public. We had discussion groups and we took advantage of these rich dialogues to polish the presentations. During 2020 we were able to have online forums with the support of CETI (Comunidad de Estudios Teológicos Interdisciplinarios). These conversation forums enabled us to continue presenting these chapters to a new Latin American audience and to continue improving them as a result of this dialogue.

Given the specific characteristics of each chapter, it is difficult to place them in a sequential order. Nevertheless, there is some sense of progress. In order to achieve *inclusio*, the first and the last chapters are reflections based on the Protestant Reformation. The second and third chapters focus on God and the gospel respectively. The fourth and fifth chapters concentrate on Latin American hermeneutics. From the sixth to the tenth chapter different aspects of the gospel are developed as that good news which emerges in the reflection from Latin America. What follows is a brief summary of each chapter.

Daniel Salinas offers us a panoramic overview of how different Protestant versions of the Reformation arrived in Latin America. That same Reformation movement passed through distinct processes of change through the centuries. The versions of the Reformation that came to us reflect that same dynamic. Without a doubt, the type of Protestantism which came to Latin America toward the end of the nineteenth century is a product of this transformation. It also shows that the results of the Reformation do not need to be the same as those that occurred in other contexts and historical periods.

Nelson Morales then shows us that, together with the gospel that reached our continent with the arrival of the Spanish until today, people have been forming an idea of God that is the product of the dialogue between the ideas already present in the continent, those ideas that foreigners brought here, plus new ideas that have been forged and developed within the Latin American context. He proposes contrasting these ideas of God with those that emerge from a more careful reading of the biblical text. He exhorts us to consider these images, in particular that of an angry God, when we proclaim the gospel of the kingdom of God.

Sadrac Meza offers an analysis of the essential components of the concept of gospel. To achieve this, he suggests six criteria to define the gospel. With these in mind, he presents a gospel that is christological, soteriological, and deontological. This way of defining the gospel then permits us to evaluate affirmations such as "the gospel is arriving in Latin America for the first time."

In the next chapter, Javier Ortega analyzes 1 Corinthians 11:2–16 and 14:34–37 with clarity and depth. He shows that leadership by women in the church is both possible and beneficial for the community of believers. His exegesis incorporates many different disciplines to uncover the past and to explain the present. From this analysis, he affirms the entire Bible as good news from Latin America.

Juan José Barreda offers a similar exegesis, but he concentrates on Matthew 19:1–12. By utilizing a variety of biblical disciplines, he presents an interpretation of the repudiation of a woman in that context that shows a more just way to face the real-life challenges of contemporary marriage. At its most basic level, he proposes a "natural" reading of the Scriptures and uses the study of this text as an example of the benefits of this contextual hermeneutic.

Ruth Padilla DeBorst emphasizes that the gospel does not separate us from our social reality. On the contrary, the church is or should be a school for the double citizenship that believers in Jesus have. The church as a community of believers demonstrates their heavenly citizenship through actions, contributing to the common good of those who live near them. Thus, they are active citizens who demonstrate the great breadth of Jesus's good news.

Dinorah Méndez presents the fruits of her research on church leadership. Although her research dealt with Mexico, the results transfer well to evangelical church leadership in many parts of Latin America. She demonstrates that, sadly, there is a recurring incongruity and intolerance that tends to follow the social leadership patterns around them, without showing clearly the biblical distinctives of Christian service, a Christian servant-leadership that should be a part of the good news of Jesus.

Darío López guides us into understanding the phenomenon of evangelical participation in politics. He especially examines the unexpected involvement in the public square by the most conservative of the evangelical churches, those that are most opposed to democracy. He explores their comprehension of democracy and citizenship within a context that hopes that dialogue, tolerance, and respect might be the guiding principles of all social participants. This chapter clearly shows that this sector of evangelicals does not practice these essential principles in the Latin American democracies that are every day more open and pluralistic.

Marcelo Vargas analyzes the implications of the gospel from an indigenous perspective. He exhorts us to be alert to the invisibility of the contributions that the Latin American indigenous reflections usually have in theological and ecclesiastical dialogues. This invisibility goes hand in hand with a Western narrative that frequently is not able to connect with our Latin American reality. This indigenous lens, for example, is much more sensitive to ecological topics and contributes other kinds of questions and reflections to this dialogue. It is a call to decolonize Christianity.

Víctor Morales presents a theological reflection on ecology. He seeks to create consciousness among us Latin American evangelicals about our responsibility to care for the world created by God. Our lifestyle is intimately connected to the earth. To deny this fact has led to its alarming degradation. In addition, Morales offers suggestions on how to interpret this task and about our relationship with our surroundings in light of the good news of our Lord Jesus Christ with a Latin American touch.

Finally, to close this *inclusio*, Rafael Zaracho challenges us to carry on a Reformation that needs to be continually reformed. He invites us to cherish our rich biblical, historical, and theological traditions that have developed in and from our communities of faith. As disciples, we are called to evaluate the "new," the "old," and the "scandalous" of our theological tradition or others in and from our participation in discernment circles. It is an invitation to assume our personal and community responsibility to discern "adequate" ways of knowing and following Jesus in our journey in community. In this discernment process as communities of faith, the invitation is to be open to the permanent guidance and continuous work of the Holy Spirit to transform us into communities of grace and reconciliation.

1

Latin America Protestant History

J. Daniel Salinas

The five hundredth anniversary of the Protestant Reformation in Europe was widely celebrated throughout Latin America. Academic talks were presented in universities and seminaries, and local churches preached sermons on the "*solas*" and showed films depicting the life and witness of Martin Luther. Does this interest demonstrate that Latin American Protestants are consciously taking on a Reformed identity? Were those celebrations a clear example of the influence of the Reformation on the Protestant church in our continent? This chapter is an attempt to analyze the reception of the Reformation by Latin American Protestants and its influence in the complex religious environment of our countries.

Preliminary Considerations

The chronological gap between the Reformation of the sixteenth century and the arrival of Protestantism to our coasts in the nineteenth century should be considered an important factor for correctly understanding the different versions of Protestantism that arrived. During those three centuries, what the Reformers began in Europe passed through processes of assimilation, purification, and systematization that led to the appearance of different versions and expressions of the Reformed faith. The transplant of heterodox groups to the Spanish and Portuguese colonies brought with it an abundance of religious options. With assistance from local dissidents, they were able to become established in Latin America. From the very beginning, the Protestant influence had little relationship to its numerical presence. Latin American religious historiography recognizes that the Protestant contribution to society from the beginning of the republican period in the continent cannot be ignored.[1]

Together with this, more recent research is changing the historical models and demonstrates that the Protestant presence in the Latin American continent has a polygenesis, that is, multiple origins. For example, the Mexican historian Carlos Mondragón distinguishes between endogenous and exogenous elements in the Protestant advance in the continent. Regarding this, Mondragón says:

> It is necessary to distinguish between: 1) the doctrines, 2) the bearers of the message, and 3) those who propagated Protestantism. Some Protestants arrived in Latin America before the institution of Protestantism and its Churches. In this way, Protestant ideas frequently preceded the professional missionaries of these Churches. The diversity of historical experiences that took place in each country regarding how Protestant ideas arrived and were extended makes any generalization quite difficult.[2]

Given the influence of the Monroe Doctrine that began in 1823, the most common Protestant expression that arrived came from the United States. There were some European attempts, such as Anglicans in the Southern Cone and, somewhat later, the Mennonites, but their influence was limited to this geographical region. The Protestants who arrived from the United States brought with them doctrinal versions that had little in common with the European Reformation of the sixteenth century. Protestants from the North had experienced the Revolutionary War, the Civil War, revivals, and the emergence of millennialism and fundamentalism, among other movements. Each one of these processes diversely affected the version of evangelicalism that was exported from the United States to their neighbors to the south. Of course, Latin America witnessed the arrival of groups that did not agree in their places of origin and continued their controversies in our lands.

---

1. See, for example, Alfonso López Michelsen, *La estirpe calvinista de nuestras instituciones políticas* (Bogotá: LEGIS, 2006); Virginia Garrard-Burnett et al., eds., *The History of Religions in Latin America* (New York: Cambridge University Press, 2016).

2. Carlos Mondragón, "Protestantes y protestantismo en América Latina: Reflexiones en torno a la variedad de experiencias en su introducción," Fraternidad Teológica Latinoamericana, 2005, accessed 11 June 2020, http://www.cenpromex.org.mx/revista_ftl/ftl/textos/carlos_mondragon.htm.

Protestant Mission in Latin America

When Protestants arrived to stay in Latin America, Spain had already dominated our land for almost four centuries. During this colonial period, the crown and the governors in the colonies were charged with making the borders impermeable to heterodox ideas. The Inquisition was efficient in its function of persecuting, condemning, and executing dissidents. Spain proudly rose up as a zealous defender of the Catholic faith and quickly began to mix culture and religious identity, a mixture used as the principal argument for their unifying campaign. The crown and its representatives in these lands promoted and imposed the idea that every Spanish subject was Roman Catholic by birth. There was no room for a different identity.

The first missionaries who came with proselytizing purposes faced an apparently homogeneous culture, closed to new ideas and a staunch defender of the status quo. Except for some liberals and freemasons who saw in the Protestant cause a possible anti-Catholic ally, everybody else believed the official propaganda against the recently arrived missionaries. Direct opposition, through all means possible, and violent and legal persecution, including fatal attacks which produced the first Protestant martyrs in the continent,[3] accompanied the beginning of Protestant work. The planting of heterogeneous ideas in soil hardened by four centuries of harsh Spanish domination was not going to be easy. Nevertheless, just as the drip, drip, drip of water makes a crack in hard marble, missionary perseverance and tenacity were able to sow the seed of the gospel, although the majority of these early sowers of the gospel passed on to glory without seeing the fruit of their labors.

The participants in the Panama Missionary Congress of 1916 saw in the ideas of the Protestant Reformation the answer to the religious and social challenges in Latin America. They understood that the Reformation should not only affect the official religion of Roman Catholicism. For example,

> To maintain perspective here, it must be taken into account that the Roman Catholic Church in Latin America profited little from the Reformation, being the projection of national bodies that reacted from the prospect of religious freedom to the excesses of the Inquisition. Intellectually, most of the clergy languish in the conceptions of the middle ages. Even the most moderate wing of the loyal modernist movement among European Roman Catholics

---

3. For example, eight Baptists were assassinated in Melcamaya, Bolivia, on 8 August 1949. See Mortimer Arias, "El protestantismo en Bolivia," in *Historia General de la Iglesia en América Latina: Perú, Bolivia y Ecuador*, eds. E. Dussel et al. (Salamanca: Sígueme, 1987), 410.

has failed to gain a hearing either from laity or clergy, so that the thinking men are without any program to point the way for them to be at once Christians and yet true to the laws of the mind and to the accepted facts of modern knowledge with which their best institutions of higher learning are abreast.[4]

Members of the Committee on Cooperation in Latin America (CCLA) proposed an agenda that would recover the Reformation for Latin America through their congresses and programs. They visualized this having a positive effect beyond church life which would reach all aspects of society. They hoped that the Reformed faith would produce "the bringing of the whole life of the individual and the entirety of society under the sway of Christ."[5] This included both the private and public proclamation of the gospel, but also the "demonstration" of the gospel message in public policies, religious and state-sponsored education, literary production, Christian service, and in other areas of social and ecclesiastical life.

From the very beginning, there was an awareness that the version of the Reformation that arrived not only came with the first generations of Reformers, but also included the great revivals of the eighteenth and nineteenth centuries, a version with a renewed "aggressive power of Protestantism."[6] Thomas Liggett at CELA II (Conferencia Evangelica Latinoamericana) in 1960 identified "post-Reformation movements such as German pietism and the evangelical awakening in England" as the sources of greatest impact in the origins of the Protestant movement in Latin America. Liggett added the influence of "an evangelical pietist impulse" from the United States and "a great number of new movements, including a considerable number with Pentecostal or 'free' characteristics."[7]

Together with these influences, it was understood that Protestantism needed to continuously renew itself. In the words of Gonzalo Báez Camargo, "one of the greatest glories of Protestantism is its ability to examine itself, to criticize itself, to renew itself, to constantly reorganize its experiences, to

---

4. Committee on Cooperation in Latin America, *Christian Work in Latin America*, vol. 1 (New York: The Missionary Movement of the United States and Canada, 1917), 139.

5. Committee on Cooperation in Latin America, *Christian Work in Latin America*, 140.

6. Committee on Cooperation in Latin America, 150.

7. Conferencia Evangelica Latinoamericana, *Cristo: la Esperanza para América Latina – Ponencias, informes, comentarios de la Segunda Conferencia Evangélica Latinoamericana, 20 de julio a 6 de agosto de 1961, Lima, Perú* (Buenos Aires: Confederación Evangélica del Rio de la Plata, 1962), 59.

reevaluate itself in light of the face of Christ."⁸ At the Havana Congress of 1929, this process was called the "Latinization of the Gospel," which led Latin American Protestants to identify themselves with the Spanish Reformers and with other Latin backgrounds in Europe. For example, the writers of the Declaración de la Primera Conferencia Evangélica Latinoamericana (CELA I) stated:

> As Latin Americans, we cannot forget that we are heirs of the Protestant tradition in the Spain of previous periods, the Spain of Casiodoro de Reina and Cipriano de Valera, who in the sixteenth century gave us the Spanish version of the Bible that we still meditate on in our homes and churches. This is that Spain that gave us so many others from the Golden Age of Hispanic Christianity who found and confessed their faith in Jesus Christ, some even dying for their faith.⁹

Midway through the twentieth century, Latin American Protestants understood that their churches were heirs of the European Reformation of the sixteenth century, and of the developments of later centuries. Although the larger influences were from the North Atlantic in their origins, Latin American Protestants looked to rediscover the Latino element in Reformation history in order to counter the propaganda of their opponents who accused them of adopting foreign cultural values. This did not mean that there was a consensus regarding the identity of Latin American Protestants. Their polygenesis created a certain amount of confusion. In the words of José Miguez Bonino, the question was whether they were "ecumenical or evangelical, CLAI or CONELA, right-wing or left-wing, evangelicals or liberationists; third ways were not acceptable."¹⁰

---

8. Gonzalo Báez-Camargo, *Hacia la renovación religiosa en Hispano-América: Resumen e interpretación del Congreso Evangélico Hispano-Americano de la Habana* (Mexico City: Casa Unida de Publicaciones, 1930), 26.

9. Conferencia Evangelica Latinoamericana, *El Cristianismo Evangélico en la América Latina: Informe y resoluciones de la Primera Conferencia Evangélica Latinoamericana, 18 al 30 de julio de 1949* (Buenos Aires: La Aurora, 1949), 10.

10. José Miguez Bonino, *Rostros del Protestantismo Latinoamericano* (Buenos Aires: Nueva Creación, 1995), 50. An English version exists as *Faces of Jesus: Latin American Christologies* (Eugene: Wipf and Stock, 1998).

The Social Aspect of the Reformation

The sixteenth-century European Protestant Reformation, in all of its variants, had an impact on political, social, and economic life, and not just religious life in the countries where they were found. Nevertheless, when the Reformation ideas took root in our lands, four centuries later, that holistic emphasis had been reduced to spiritual and religious areas, leaving broader concerns to one side. The element that was most lacking and which produced most ambivalence in the Reformation versions that arrived in Latin America was the issue of social and political participation. Emilio Antonio Núñez explains that

> many North American missionaries who came to Latin America between 1900 and 1940 were premillennialists in their eschatology, pietists in their understanding of Christianity, and separatists in their basic attitude toward ecclesiastical bodies and toward society in general. One of the principal characteristics of "faith missions" in our countries, generally, was their reluctance to accept their social responsibility. They were a product, to a high degree, of the "Great Reversal" in North American evangelicalism.[11]

Mexican researcher Carlos Mondragón analyzed this move in Protestants from "revolutionary activism to social lethargy."[12] Another Mexican scholar, Leopoldo Cervantes-Ortiz, acknowledges that these Protestantisms were supposedly "apolitical," but in fact were allied with dictatorships in Central and South America.[13] In the 1960s and 1970s Iglesia y Sociedad (ISAL)[14] and liberation theologies appeared with clear proposals for social and political activities for Protestants. These groups were repressed from the outside, in the context of the Cold War, and from within by conservative organizations, both Catholic and Protestant, that saw in them an undesirable mix of faith

---

11. Emilio Antonio Núñez, *Teología y misión: Perspectivas desde América Latina* (San José: Visión Mundial Internacional, 1995), 263.

12. Carlos Mondragón, "México: De la militancia revolucionaria al letargo social," in *De la marginación al compromiso: Los evangélicos y la política en América Latina*, ed. René Padilla (Buenos Aires, FTL, 1991), 61–76.

13. Leopoldo Cervantes-Ortiz, "The Protestant Reformation and Social Justice in Latin America," *The Ecumenical Review* 69, no. 2 (2017): 259.

14. For a good overview of the perspectives of ISAL, see Leopoldo Cervantes-Ortiz, "Génesis de la nueva teología protestante latinoamericana (1949–1970)," *Cuadernos de Teología* 23 (2004): 221–250. See also Daniel Salinas, *Teología con alma Latina: El pensamiento evangélico en el siglo XX* (Lima: Ediciones Puma, 2018), 105–124.

and politics. What would have happened if the original Protestant proposals had been thoroughly applied in our continent?[15]

As an example of repression from the outside, Juan Pablo Somiedo García describes the reaction of the United States government toward liberation theology:

> Although it might seem paradoxical, the first criticism of Liberation Theology did not come from the Vatican, but from the Rockefeller Report in 1969, one year after Vice President Nixon's trip throughout Latin America. This Report maintained that the Church was no longer a trustworthy ally for the U.S.A., nor was it a guarantee for social stability in the continent. It had been transformed into a dangerous center for possible revolution. It also recommended countering the influence of the Catholic Church with the influence of Protestant churches or sects closer to the interests of the United States in Latin America.[16]

A decade later, in May 1980, writings were being developed in secret that formed the basis of the Santa Fe Document. In fact, this document became the foundation of the ethical-religious doctrine for Latin America of the Reagan administration. The document was suggestively titled "A New Inter-American Policy for the Eighties." Regarding the topic of religion, it recommended "combatting Liberation Theology through every possible means and control[ling] mass social media to counter the bad image of the United States in the region."[17] In a similar way, it maintained that liberation theologians used this theology as a political weapon against private property and productive capitalism.

As a consequence, the Institute on Religion and Democracy was created in April 1981 to unify all of the evangelical churches in Latin America and

---

15. To evaluate the supposed "apolitical" posture of Latin American Protestants, with examples of those who actively participated in politics, see Lindy "Luis" Scott, *La sal de la tierra: Una historia socio-política de los evangélicos en la ciudad de México (1964–1991)* (Mexico City: Editorial Kyrios, 1991). The English version of this book is Lindy Scott, *Salt of the Earth: A Socio-Political History of Evangelical Protestants in Mexico City (1964–1991)* (Mexico City: Editorial Kyrios, 1991). For a case study of the direct influence of Protestants in politics, see Washington Padilla, *La iglesia y los dioses modernos: Historia del protestantismo en el Ecuador* (Quito: Corporación Editora Nacional, 1989).

16. Juan Pablo Somiedo García, "La influencia de la geopolítica estadounidense en la teología de la liberación latinoamericana en el periodo 1960–1990," *Geopolíticas* 5, no. 1 (2014): 87.

17. Documento Santa Fé I (Indice), (http://www.desaparecidos.org/nuncamas/web/document/docstfe1_00intro.htm).

to fund their evangelization. In similar fashion, it supported financially the most conservative Catholic archbishops, including Miguel Obando y Bravo, archbishop of Managua.[18]

The Santa Fe Document stated: "The United States foreign policy should begin to counter (not to react against) Liberation Theology . . . Christian than communist."[19]

An example of internal repression was the Catholic Sacred Congregation for the Doctrine of the Faith led by Cardinal Joseph Ratzinger from 1981 to 2005. In 1984, the Congregation published the document "Instruction on Certain Aspects of the 'Theology of Liberation'" with the explicit purpose

> to draw the attention of pastors, theologians, and all the faithful to the deviations, and risks of deviation, damaging to the faith and to Christian living, that are brought about by certain forms of liberation theology which use, in an insufficiently critical manner, concepts borrowed from various currents of Marxist thought.[20]

Therefore, the Protestant legacy that we have received has been partial and limited, supported by dichotomies that arose during the three intervening centuries between the European Reformation and the arrival of Protestants in Latin America. Nevertheless, the vein of a holistic understanding of the gospel was not totally lost. It continued to emerge in a variety of ways. For example, the Colombian Milton Mejía, who analyzed Calvin's legacy, recognizes that upon

> reviewing the way that Calvin and the Reformed Protestant tradition led to theological and social science, we learn that the study and interpretation of the Bible with a pastoral focus on all society have been central. They attempted to provide a response to the problems and situations of their society and church in their time.[21]

---

18. Somiedo García, "La influencia de la geopolítica estadounidense," 87.

19. Documento Santa Fé I (Indice), (http://www.desaparecidos.org/nuncamas/web/document/docstfe1_00intro.htm).

20. Sacred Congregation for the Doctrine of the Faith, "Instruction on Certain Aspects of the 'Theology of Liberation,'" https://www.vatican.va/roman_curia/congregations/cfaith/documents/rc_con_cfaith_doc_19840806_theology-liberation_en.html.

21. Milton Mejía, "Una aproximación a la forma de hacer teología protestante reformada," in *Teología reformada y desafíos contemporáneos*, eds. César Carhuachín and Milton Mejía (Barranquilla: Corporación Universitaria and CLAI, 2017), 178.

Mejía adds:

> Based on this tradition and experience, we have learned to make Reformed theology from our church and social reality in Colombia and Latin America in order to respond to the local and global problems that we experience. Today, when we are celebrating 500 years of the Reformation, we face the challenge of renewing our tradition and continuing to create theology from the Protestant perspective. To achieve this, we need to form our pastors and church leaders who are involved in the experience of theological production and with a commitment to social transformation in our educational and church communities and in our society.[22]

As Mejía proposes, this implies that we recreate the tradition we have received but from within our contemporary context, in order "to give an answer to the new situations and problems that we experience in the church and in society."[23] What Mejía proposes can be implemented only in a church willing "to live in a process of permanent reformation." This is easy to say but difficult to put into practice, because it goes against the stability that churches value.

From within the Lutheran tradition, the social legacy of the Reformation has been maintained. At the seminar workshop that took place in Lima in July 1985, Milton Schwantes, in his closing speech, alluded to Luther's sermon on good works (1518), and encouraged the participants to recover "an infrequently used Lutheran tradition" referring to effective social work. Among other things, he said:

> The theology of the cross does not only speak about the salvific work of God for us. It also speaks about people, about history. The theology of the cross implies, inevitably, a way of understanding history. When it is revealed through weakness, our God draws near to the weak, and takes the form of a slave, born in a manger, and dying in the midst of the marginalized. His incarnation took place in a specific historical and social place and time. God gives special attention to the poor and enters into conflict with the strong.[24]

---

22. Mejía, "Una aproximación a la forma de hacer teología protestante reformada," 178.

23. Mejía, 180.

24. Milton Schwantes, "Anotaciones sobre la teología luterana en América Latina," in *Acción Social: Obra de la iglesia luterana – Informe del II Seminario-Taller, Lima, 7 al 13 de julio de 1985* (Lima: Lutheran World Relief, 1985), 150.

Also referring to Luther, Sidney H. Rooy concludes that the work of evangelization is based on

> all proclamation of the gospel and every act of service realized through the church.... Luther never tires of affirming that the church that does not demonstrate with its life and does not witness with its mouth to the love of God in Jesus Christ is the door of demons and not the door of salvation.[25]

There is an additional example in which the social aspect of the Reformation remains active. This comes from the Wesleyan Methodist tradition. The Guatemalan theologian Federico R. Meléndez encourages his readers that, to follow in the Wesleyan tradition, "it is necessary to recover the vision and the central place of the individual in God's economy and in the human economy." For Meléndez, this should lead us to formulate certain questions:

> What is the message of holiness that we should proclaim in our globalized world? How can we continue to be holy in a world full of injustices and contradictions? What is our role as Christians who face the challenges of Mammon, the Greek god of wealth and of the consumer society that distorts our value as people? What do we do when our world is bowed down and submerged in poverty, especially in our Latin American countries? Is there a place for an economy with a human face?[26]

Meléndez ends by encouraging the church in Latin America

> to develop a holistic plan of action in which our greatest effort is concentrated in responding to the great needs of our people. The result needs to be a sanctified church, filled with God's Spirit, that puts all of its talents, resources, and services to the benefit of those who most need them.[27]

---

25. Sidney H. Rooy, *Lutero y la misión: Teología y práctica de la misión en Martín Lutero* (St. Louis: Concordia, 2005), 91.

26. Federico R. Meléndez, *Ética y economía: El legado de Juan Wesley a la iglesia en América Latina* (Buenos Aires: Kairos, 2006), 104.

27. Meléndez, *Ética y economía*, 136.

A Recent Alternate Historical View

In spite of all that Latin American Protestants have applied from the sixteenth-century Reformation teachings, there are those who claim that the Reformed gospel never reached our lands. For example, the Dominican Baptist pastor Miguel Núñez has written that "the gospel preached by the Reformers is not the same as the one that our Latin American countries received." Núñez adds that "the Reformation never affected this region of the world" and, therefore, Latin America needs to be evangelized again. The fact that Núñez draws on to support his affirmation is that our continent has not experienced the economic and social benefits realized by European and North American countries. According to his interpretation, the Reformation was the main cause of the differences between the South and the North.[28]

Núñez is right when he states that the versions of the gospel that reached us were not the same as those of the sixteenth century. Nevertheless, his argument contains many historical and sociological fallacies. In the first place, the Protestant Reformation was only one of many social factors that Europe experienced during that century. Economic analyses that attributed to the Protestant ethic the greater economic and social prosperity of the countries that adopted the Calvinist principle compared with those that did not are now considered obsolete. Europe was in a state of transformation and revolution even before the sixteenth century and continued in this process for a few more centuries. Without a doubt, the Reformation contributed to this process, but it was not the only factor, nor was it the most relevant.[29]

It is a simplistic analysis to compare the social and economic situation of Latin America with that of Europe and conclude that the differences are due to the fact that the effects of the Protestant Reformation never arrived in Latin America. The colonial powers are today enjoying the results of the pillage they committed upon the countries they conquered. This was illustrated when an African friend of mine visited Belgium. When she asked what supported the Belgian economy, she was told that, among other things, it was diamonds. When she asked where in Belgium the diamond mines were, she was told that all the mines were in Africa. This is the situation today with a capitalist commercial colonization that favors those in the Global North and leaves the countries of the South in ruins. José Míguez de Bonino has described it like this:

---

28. Miguel Núñez, *El poder de la Palabra para transformar una nación: Un llamado bíblico e histórico a la iglesia latinoamericana* (Medellín: Poiema, 2017), 5–17.

29. For a good overview of medieval European history, see Justo L. González, *Historia del Cristianismo*, vol. 1 (Miami: Spanish House, 1994), from chapter 29 to the end.

Latin American underdevelopment is the shadow of the North Atlantic development; the development of one world is built upon the underdevelopment of the third world. The basic categories needed to understand our history are not development and underdevelopment, but rather domination and dependency. This is the heart of the problem.[30]

It is clear that geographical, historical, and sociological factors, among others, have also played a role in the differences. For example, Tim Marshall, in his bestseller *Prisoners of Geography: Ten Maps That Tell You Everything You Need to Know about Global Politics*, shows that geographical factors have helped the countries of northern Europe to have larger and more stable economies than countries in the southern part of the continent.[31] This analysis is made without any appeal to the changes that the Reformation produced in the sixteenth century.

There is another problem in Núñez's analysis that we also find in other proposals. They begin with the premise that Latin America should be at the same level as Europe and the United States. These people shake their heads, but they are never able to comprehend why we Latin Americans are not more like Europeans or North Americans.[32] This interpretation does not acknowledge the historical and social differences between the continents that are compared. On the other hand, one should not expect a European religious phenomenon to produce similar results in Latin America to those produced in its original context.

It cannot be denied that the gospel has reached and affected Latin America. Whether it is the medieval pre-Trent Catholicism or the version of the religious orders, or the gospel of the Protestant waves, different flavors of the gospel have reached us. Núñez's argument does not do justice to what missionaries have done throughout the centuries of Christian presence in our lands. We need to better understand our own context in order to not become a mere copy of Christians in the North. The goal of evangelization, as the documents of the 1916 Panama Congress expressed, is not to "North Americanize," nor to impose imported models.

---

30. José Míguez Bonino, *La fe en busca de la eficacia* (Salamanca: Sígueme, 1977), 39–40.

31. Tim Marshall, *Prisoners of Geography: Ten Maps That Tell You Everything You Need to Know about Global Politics* (London: Elliot & Thompson, 2016), especially pp. 89–113.

32. I explain this in detail in *Latin American Evangelical Theology in the 1970s: The Golden Decade* (Leiden: Brill, 2009), ch. 2.

In Núñez's words, an idealization of what the Protestant Reformation achieved in Europe can also be observed. We Protestants like to narrate our history and sometimes turn it into hagiography, where we emphasize its positive characteristics and omit the negative ones. The historiography of the period reminds us that the reality was never so simple. The Reformation did indeed bring benefits, but it also caused many problems, especially wars, persecution, and destruction. Even in present times, religious tensions continue in various European countries, tensions that arose in the sixteenth century. In the words of Colombian Pablo Moreno,

> in today's Europe, we can still appreciate grandiose museums, church buildings, monuments, and enormous libraries of the Protestant Reformation, but very little remains of the enthusiastic and dynamic faith of the Protestant communities of the sixteenth century. Nevertheless, it is worthwhile to ask certain questions. For example, are we asking of the Reformation and the Reformers more than they can deliver? To what extent are we ignoring the historical processes that have taken place in the assimilation of this legacy in England and the United States in the seventeenth and nineteenth centuries? . . . As we study the Reformation, we must avoid melancholy, as if it were a finished product that has got lost over the years. On the contrary, it is better to understand it as the beginning of a movement of the Church always reforming without ending, which continues with the efforts and contribution of each generation.[33]

I agree with Núñez that, to a great extent, the gospel has been limited to what takes place within the four walls of churches. It is clear that his pastoral heart has led him to desire a more palpable effect of the gospel in society. But the proposal that the solution must be another imported religious version that tries to reproduce in our land foreign social phenomena does not acknowledge what, for almost two centuries, Latin American Protestants have achieved in "Latin Americanizing" the gospel message. Today we have a local and contextualized holistic mission of the church. We do not need our spiritual siblings from the North, albeit with good intentions, to come in the twenty-first century with their prepackaged version of what they consider to be the gospel

---

33. Pablo Moreno, "Reforma de Reformas," in *500 años de las reformas protestantes, 1517–2017: Discusiones interdisciplinarias*, eds. Atahualpa Hernández M. and Fernando A. Sanmiguel M. (Bogotá: Corporación Honorable Presbiterio Central, Iglesia Presbiteriana de Colombia, and Iglesia Luterana de Colombia, 2017), 142.

that Latin America needs today. This, in addition to not respecting our Latin American theology, is an attempt to maintain the theological, ideological, and ecclesiastical dependency that has caused so much damage to the Protestant presence in our Latin American continent.

Conclusion

Latin American Protestants have seen themselves, and continue to see themselves, as heirs of the Protestant Reformation. This identification has different degrees of importance, from those who include "Reformed" in the name of their denomination or local church, to those who barely understand what the Reformed heritage means. Many have had to pay a high price for this legacy. From their beginning, the Protestant minority has recognized the need to "Latin Americanize" the European proposal. They have also understood that the Reformation, more than a historical event, should be a movement. This is expressed in the idea of a church in permanent reformation, which avoids stagnation, a reformation that becomes a new reality in each generation, that always responds to the new challenges to the faith and to Christian life. We now have an abundant theological, doctrinal, and pastoral production, born in our Latin American soil, from which we have been able to nurture our reflection today, but we cannot rest on our laurels. The challenge is to continue being relevant, committed to the aspirations of our people, and in submission to the authority of the Word and to the sovereignty of God.

References

Arias, Mortimer. "El protestantismo en Bolivia." In *Historia General de la Iglesia en América Latina: Perú, Bolivia y Ecuador*, edited by E. Dussel et al. 405–414, Salamanca: Sígueme, 1987.

Báez-Camargo, Gonzalo. *Hacia la renovación religiosa en Hispano-América: Resumen e interpretación del Congreso Evangélico Hispano-Americano de la Habana*. Mexico City: Casa Unida de Publicaciones, 1930.

Cervantes-Ortiz, Leopoldo. "Génesis de la nueva teología protestante latinoamericana (1949–1970)." *Cuadernos de Teología* 23 (2004): 221–250.

———. "The Protestant Reformation and Social Justice in Latin America." *The Ecumenical Review* 69, no. 2 (2017): 249–259.

Committee on Cooperation in Latin America. *Christian Work in Latin America*. Vol. 1. New York: The Missionary Movement of the United States and Canada, 1917.

Conferencia Evangelica Latinoamericana. *El Cristianismo Evangélico en la América Latina: Informe y resoluciones de la Primera Conferencia Evangélica Latinoamericana, 18 al 30 de julio de 1949.* Buenos Aires: La Aurora, 1949.

———. *Cristo: la Esperanza para América Latina – Ponencias, informes, comentarios de la Segunda Conferencia Evangélica Latinoamericana, 20 de julio a 6 de agosto de 1961, Lima, Perú.* Buenos Aires: Confederación Evangélica del Rio de la Plata, 1962.

Documento Santa Fé I (Indice), (http://www.desaparecidos.org/nuncamas/web/document/docstfe1_00intro.htm).

Garrard-Burnett, Virginia, et al., eds. *The History of Religions in Latin America.* New York: Cambridge University Press, 2016.

González, Justo L. *Historia del Cristianismo.* Vol. 1. Miami: Spanish House, 1994.

López Michelsen, Alfonso. *La estirpe calvinista de nuestras instituciones políticas.* Bogotá: LEGIS, 2006.

Marshall, Tim. *Prisoners of Geography: Ten Maps That Tell You Everything You Need to Know about Global Politics.* London: Elliot & Thompson, 2016.

Mejía, Milton. "Una aproximación a la forma de hacer teología protestante reformada." In *Teología reformada y desafíos contemporáneos,* edited by César Carhuachín and Milton Mejía, 155–182. Barranquilla: Corporación Universitaria and CLAI, 2017.

Meléndez, Federico R. *Ética y economía: El legado de Juan Wesley a la iglesia en América Latina.* Buenos Aires: Kairos, 2006.

Miguez Bonino, José. *Faces of Jesus: Latin American Christologies.* Eugene: Wipf and Stock, 1998.

———. *La fe en busca de la eficacia.* Salamanca: Sígueme, 1977.

———. *Rostros del Protestantismo Latinoamericano.* Buenos Aires: Nueva Creación, 1995.

Mondragón, Carlos. "México: De la militancia revolucionaria al letargo social." In *De la marginación al compromiso: Los evangélicos y la política en América Latina,* edited by René Padilla, 61–76. Buenos Aires: FTL, 1991.

———. "Protestantes y protestantismo en América Latina: Reflexiones en torno a la variedad de experiencias en su introducción." Fraternidad Teológica Latinoamericana, 2005. Accessed 11 June 2020. http://www.cenpromex.org.mx/revista_ftl/ftl/textos/carlos_mondragon.htm.

Moreno, Pablo. "Reforma de Reformas." In *500 años de las reformas protestantes, 1517–2017: Discusiones interdisciplinarias,* edited by Atahualpa Hernández M. and Fernando A. Sanmiguel M., 139–158. Bogotá: Corporación Honorable Presbiterio Central, Iglesia Presbiteriana de Colombia, and Iglesia Luterana de Colombia, 2017.

Núñez, Emilio Antonio. *Teología y misión: Perspectivas desde América Latina.* San José: Visión Mundial Internacional, 1995.

Núñez, Miguel. *El poder de la Palabra para transformar una nación: Un llamado bíblico e histórico a la iglesia latinoamericana.* Medellín: Poiema, 2017.

Padilla, Washington. *La iglesia y los dioses modernos: Historia del protestantismo en el Ecuador.* Quito: Corporación Editora Nacional, 1989.

Rooy, Sidney H. *Lutero y la misión: Teología y práctica de la misión en Martín Lutero.* St. Louis: Concordia, 2005.

Sacred Congregation for the Doctrine of the Faith. "Instruction on Certain Aspects of the 'Theology of Liberation.'" https://www.vatican.va/roman_curia/congregations/cfaith/documents/rc_con_cfaith_doc_19840806_theology-liberation_en.html.

Salinas, Daniel. *Latin American Evangelical Theology in the 1970s: The Golden Decade.* Leiden: Brill, 2009.

———. *Teología con alma Latina: El pensamiento evangélico en el siglo XX.* Lima: Ediciones Puma, 2018.

Schwantes, Milton. "Anotaciones sobre la teología luterana en América Latina." In *Acción Social: Obra de la iglesia luterana – Informe del II Seminario-Taller, Lima, 7 al 13 de julio de 1985*, 147–57. Lima: Lutheran World Relief, 1985.

Scott, Lindy "Luis." *La sal de la tierra: Una historia socio-política de los evangélicos en la ciudad de México (1964–1991).* Mexico City: Editorial Kyrios, 1991.

———. *Salt of the Earth: A Socio-Political History of Evangelical Protestants in Mexico City (1964–1991).* Mexico City: Editorial Kyrios, 1991.

Somiedo García, Juan Pablo. "La influencia de la geopolítica estadounidense en la teología de la liberación latinoamericana en el periodo 1960–1990." *Geopolíticas* 5, no. 1 (2014): 79–98.

2

Images of God in Latin America

Nelson R. Morales Fredes

At the end of the fifteenth century, America witnessed the arrival of sailors in ships and, together with them, a cross. Soon, new waves of Europeans brought with them their faith and their understanding of God. As a result of that pilgrimage of Europeans, a large part of the image of God we have forged in these lands has been deeply molded by a dialogue between the ideas that they brought and the ideas that already existed in the continent. As the centuries rolled on, new visitors arrived by boat and plane from Europe and North America with new ideas and images of God that in one way or another put down roots in our lands. At the same time, other images of God emerged as a result of reflection and experiences lived out in our region. Therefore, it is difficult, if not impossible, to paint only one image of God in Latin America.

Naturally, an essential image in Latin American Christianity is that of God, creator of heaven and earth, who expresses his love toward creation through the redeeming work of his Son, who died and rose from the dead and ascended into heaven, who rules and from there will come again. This creator God is a God who shares his gifts with his people through his Spirit. At the same time, this is a God who has control over history and who guides it toward its goal. This history culminates with a new heaven and a new earth, the judgment of the wicked, the vindication of the righteous, and the establishment of an eternal kingdom in which justice and righteousness reign. This image of God has accompanied Christianity since its irruption in these latitudes. Nevertheless, throughout its history, together with this first image there have coexisted other images that have occasionally covered or hidden from our eyes the God of the Bible.

Sadly, space limits us from being exhaustive in our information. In the following sections, I will present a panorama of some images of God that are portrayed in different Christian groups throughout the length and breadth of the continent and the Caribbean. What will be presented is a typological outline of some of the recurring images of God in each group described. I strive not to mischaracterize or blur the motley image of God current in Latin America. Without a doubt, previous typologies have been helpful, such as Emilio Antonio Núñez's *El Cristo de Hispanoamérica* (1979) or those images described by John A. Mackay in his *El otro Cristo español: Un estudio de la historia espiritual de España e Hispanoamérica* (1952). In what follows, I will present an outline of the images of God in classic Roman Catholicism, in the thought of liberation theology, in the Fraternidad Teológica Latinoamericana (Latin American Theological Fellowship), in traditional evangelicalism, in neo-Pentecostalism, and in the Gospel Coalition (Coalición por el Evangelio).

Images of God in Classic Roman Catholicism

We begin with Roman Catholicism because this has been, and continues to be, the largest and oldest representation of Christianity in Latin America. A couple of decades after the arrival of Christopher Columbus in the Caribbean, the Spanish began to use the *Requerimiento* of Juan López de Palacios Rubios. In this writing, God is presented as the one and only Lord, the creator of heaven and earth and of humanity. He has delegated his authority to the Catholic Church, to the Pope, and to the Spanish monarchs. The *Requerimiento* was used to force the inhabitants of these lands to submit to the dominion of the Pope and of the Spanish monarchs. Not long after, in 1524 twelve Franciscan friars arrived to evangelize in the already battered Mexican land. In Friar Sahagún's recompilation of the conversations between these friars and indigenous leaders, an image of God is demonstrated that continues up to our times, not only in folk Catholic theology, but in Protestant theology as well. This presentation of the gospel states in its second chapter:

> you do not know the one true God by whom we all live, you do not fear nor heed him. On the contrary, every day and every night you offend him in many ways, and therefore you have earned his anger and fallen into disgrace, and he is very angry with you. For this reason, he has sent his Spanish servants and vassals to punish you and afflict you for the innumerable sins that you have fallen into.[1]

---

1. Juan Guillermo Durán and Rubén Darío García, "Los coloquios de los 'Doce Apóstoles' de México: Los primeros albores de la predicación evangélica en el Nuevo Mundo," *Revista de la Facultad de Teología de la Pontificia Católica Argentina* 34 (1979): 131–85, lines 450–56.

In both the *Requerimiento* and the *Coloquios*, God is described as the creator, kind, but irascible. If in addition to this we acknowledge the belief, already present in these latitudes, of capricious gods who must be placated with sacrifices and offerings, this image became reinforced in the unconscious collective religious mentality. José Luis Sicre affirms that this is the image of a vindictive God, who is placated by the intervention of the Virgin Mary.[2] Certainly this is not the only image of God discernible in Catholic circles, but it is the most dominant one.

This divine image is added to the one of a God who in the final judgment weighs humanity's good and evil deeds, and makes his judgment based upon which weighs more. In this way, an image of a God who is not satisfied with the sacrifice of his Son Jesus remains rooted in the collective social mentality. Jesus's work of salvation needs to be accompanied by other meritorious acts. According to this version, natural disasters, even sicknesses or personal or collective tragedies, are interpreted as punishments from God. This violent God becomes an excuse for either defending or questioning human political powers. God is recognized as the creator, but frequently is seen as distant from people.

This image of God will follow us for centuries. Even in Protestant circles, as we will see below, this idea of an angry God is so deeply rooted in Latin American cultures that it is difficult to overcome and remove it and to move toward a more biblical image of the God of Scripture. Latin American ears are almost always predisposed to hear "the anger of God" and automatically evoke this idea. Therefore, in the process of evangelization, missionary work, and discipleship, we should pay close attention to the ideas that we project and highlight, in such a way that we can maintain a balanced and biblical image. Nevertheless, there have been efforts to change this angry God image, especially in Catholic renewal circles.

Images of God in Liberation Theology (Both Catholic and Protestant)

The image of the angry God is also discernible in liberation theology's spheres of influence, in both its Catholic and Protestant versions. In early liberation circles, this image of an angry, and sometimes violent, God was linked to the suffering of the oppressed. He was frequently described as the God who wanted to free his people from out of Egypt. This is not the same image as that described in the previous section, because in the liberationist model God is not capricious.

---

2. José Luis Sicre, "El Dios de los profetas: Contra una imagen 'light' del Dios cristiano," *Sal Terrae* 76 (1988): 420.

To the contrary, the suffering of the helpless causes pain to God himself. He has demonstrated a preferential attitude to the poor. For that reason, he acts to help and liberate them, whom he considers to be the crucified of history. With this goal in mind, he first sent Jesus Christ, the liberator. Based on his sacrifice, he guides his people toward liberation. In some cases, including in public discourse, proponents have proclaimed that God supports the most explicit actions of liberation. These included Camilo Torres Restrepo in Colombia in the mid 1960s and Ernesto Cardenal in Nicaragua in the late 1970s.[3]

It is obvious that this image of God has changed greatly in the writings and thought of liberation theologians during the last decades of reflection and change in the Latin American context.[4] Oppressive forces are still present, but theological reflection has expanded its understanding of God to show that he also hears the groaning of the earth that suffers oppression. Not only people but also nature awaits the liberating action of God the Creator. In this regard, the image of God that has been portrayed most recently in liberation circles is that of God the Creator who is near, who hears the cries that have reached his ears. This clamor is not just from the poor, but from every marginalized person and community, women, and indigenous people. At the same time, he is a God who sees the suffering of his creation and expects humanity to intervene. In fact, he is a God who expects the oppressed to take concrete action. In a certain sense, he is a biased God who does not seem to receive the most privileged of the earth.

This image is more balanced than the one mentioned earlier and is also present in some segments of Latin American Catholic thought outside of liberation theology. Nevertheless, it carries the risk of distorting the image of God who not only chooses the poor, but desires the salvation of all human beings. It is a God who receives into his bosom everyone he loves. Without a doubt, he is a God of hope, because he vindicates the righteous and punishes the wicked. The ears of the Lord are indeed attentive to the cries of the suffering and he brings about justice, both now and at the end of time. He has chosen the poor, but he extends his offer to become heirs of the kingdom not only to them. He makes this offer to all those he loves. Therefore, he demands that we love everyone he loves, and that we take care of his garden where he has placed us as stewards.

---

3. See the excellent analysis of Pastor Bedolla Villaseñor, "La Teología de la Liberación: Pastoral y violencia revolucionarias," *Revista de Estudios Latinoamericanos* 64 (2017): 185–221.

4. Regarding these changes, see the solid analysis and distinct articles in Alejandro F. Botta and Pablo R. Andiñach, *The Bible and the Hermeneutics of Liberation*, Society of Biblical Literature Semeia Studies (Atlanta: Society of Biblical Literature, 2009).

Images of God in the Fraternidad Teológica Latinoamericana (FTL; Latin American Theological Fellowship)

The God who is portrayed in the groups affiliated with the Latin American Theological Fellowship (FTL) is generally similar to that described in the previous section. Similar to what has taken place in liberation theology, the FTL images of God and their emphases have changed over the years. The image is frequently of God the Creator who identifies and suffers with the afflicted. He is a God who is attentive to help every human being, and is not just about saving souls from eternal condemnation. He is a God who seeks reconciliation, not just with individuals, but with people in community. For the scholars associated with FTL, the roles of the Son and of the Spirit are essential. On the one hand, the Lord Jesus Christ is the one who brings integral, holistic salvation, but he also opens the door for the people of God to take action in bringing liberation guided by the transforming power of the Holy Spirit. The action of God through redeemed humanity is not merely political – although it can transform thoughts and actions in the political sphere; it is also redemptive and salvific. God is in control of human history and guides it toward its goal. In fact, his kingdom is expanding in concrete ways in the midst of humanity, and transcends the church, although the church is the representative and living witness of that kingdom. As James Gehman says, "The church is God's instrument to fulfill his purposes. The church is the sacrament, the sign of the presence of God in history"; its mission is worship, fellowship, service, and justice.[5]

FTL also portrays a God who is concerned about his creation, which he yearns to redeem. He demands that we who inhabit it be responsible and take care of it. In the words of James Padilla DeBorst, this is a God who is concerned about "*equi-rollo*" (equi-velopment), in a development with equity, of the entire humanity in harmony with creation. The gospel is shalom; God is a God who brings this shalom to human society by means of the actions of his people.[6]

There is always a risk in this kind of reflection. Paradoxically, it can lead to an imbalance tilted toward the urgent social and ecological concerns, in such a way that God is portrayed as more concerned about social, political, and ecological issues than he is about whole human beings. The challenge is to derive from Scripture a balanced image of God the Creator.

---

5. James A. Gehman, "Definición de la misión integral e implicaciones para la hermenéutica bíblica," *Kairós* 45, no. 2 (2009): 126–27.

6. Santiago James Padilla DeBorst, "Decolonial Integral Mission? Development and Contextualization at New Scales," *Journal of Latin American Theology* 13, no. 1 (2018): 65–75.

Images of God in Traditional Evangelicalism

In traditional Latin American evangelicalism, various images of God exist simultaneously. On the one hand, the idea of an angry God has profoundly marked Protestant thought. Within those sectors that emphasize predestination, such as Calvinists, at a popular level there persists the idea of this angry God who, in the end, decides to give salvation based on people's conduct in this life. It is an employer God, as Pablo Deiros describes him, "with an arbitrary and abusive character, who presents himself as a vindictive being, more inclined to demonstrate his ire and anger than gestures and actions of mercy and grace."[7] This image of God, in combination with natural disasters or situations of poverty or violence, leads some believers to a life of resignation before the incomprehensible designs of God. This is frequently expressed in phrases such as "What are we going to do? That's the way God wanted it?" As one of my uncles told me, "You Protestants can have a wall in your house fall down, and you just sit there with your arms crossed and do nothing, except to say, 'This was the will of God.'"

On the other hand, there is the image of a God more concerned with the salvation of people's souls than with their bodies. He is a God who provides the salvation of souls that go to heaven, but he is not very concerned about the degradation of the planet because he is going to destroy it at the end of time.

Coexisting with these two images, and becoming increasingly more common, is the image of a God who loves all people and the planet. At the same time, he is more active in human politics, he stirs up a more prophetic voice among his people, he likes neoliberal economics, and he identifies with the traditional values of Latin American families. He is a God who has heavenly handkerchiefs ready, but is usually silent when faced with the affliction of the poor or labor injustices.

Thanks be to God that not everything is bad. The God expressed in Latin American evangelicalism is a God who is near, especially in times of sorrow. He is a God who is eager to help the person in need. He is a Father who not only disciplines, but above all loves, takes care of, and provides comfort. He is a God who generally, throughout Protestant history, has identified with the person who is poor, with the widow, and with the uneducated. In this sense, he is a God who does not discriminate, but rather empowers his sons and daughters to live out their daily lives.

---

7. Pablo A. Deiros, *El mundo religioso latinoamericano* (El Paso: Casa Bautista, 2017), 475.

Images of God in Neo-Pentecostalism

Just as in the rest of the Protestant world, there exist various images of God within neo-Pentecostalism. One important conceptualization of God quite prevalent in the Pentecostal world is that of a God who changes the course of reality. This image is powerful and has had an impact in changing the fatalism that is also present in Latin American evangelicalism. He is a God who, in his love and omnipotence, responds to the fervent faith of his children who cry out in prayer. In addition, he is a God who reveals his will through the Holy Spirit by means of revelations, dreams, and powerful acts.

At the same time, one of the images that stands out is that of a God who is subordinated to humans. He is a God who is tied to the declarations and demands of leaders with spiritual power. He is a God who is obligated to fulfill the desires of people, expressed as positive pronouncements that unbind the reality that they declare. The image of God the Banker is usually associated with this image. He will financially provide for a person's economic standard of living according to the capitalistic consumer in vogue. This health and wealth gospel is principally practiced by leaders whom God has anointed with power and they, therefore, have God's anointing.

There are certain contradictions in these images. On the one hand, the first-mentioned image seems to move toward a biblical balance. The supernatural God does continue to act in the midst of his people. Therefore, we should restore this image in our proclamation of the God of Scripture. Nevertheless, on the other hand, a God who is subordinated to humanity is a distortion that causes great damage. The presence of this image is so dominant among the people in the pew that it almost competes with the image of the angry God within these circles.

Images of God in the Gospel Coalition

Although the movement known as the Gospel Coalition is relatively new in Latin America, its media and literary impact is important. Some of the images of God already mentioned can be observed in the Gospel Coalition's writings. Its strong emphasis on soteriological issues is such that it reduces the content of the gospel to issues of personal salvation at the expense of other biblical attributes of the gospel.[8] Therefore, the proclamation of the good news that the kingdom of God is at hand becomes reduced to an individualistic salvation for

---

8. For example, see various of the chapters in D. A. Carson and Timothy Keller, eds., *La centralidad del Evangelio* (Miami: Patmos, 2014), 19–20, 43, 131–55.

those who wish to believe in Jesus as their personal savior. God is portrayed as being more interested in the salvation of the individual than in the life of the community where the person lives. He is a God who lives only in the hearts of the individuals he saves. The kingdom of God is also limited to these human hearts. In this way, according to Bryan Chapell, the kingdom of God advances only from heart to heart through the proclamation and work of the individuals who constitute the church.[9]

As can be seen, the angry God is also present in this evangelistic message. In fact, in the little bit of space dedicated to the poor and marginalized, authors Don Carson and Timothy Keller, in the initial declaration in the preface to their book *La centralidad del Evangelio* (the Centrality of the Gospel), interpret the work of Christ at the cross basically in terms of "placating the anger of God." From there, they would say that we should be sensitive to the rights of the poor, those who "are in economic bankruptcy," to the point that "we should be willing to give from our resources to 'the poor who don't deserve anything' because we are the spiritually poor and we do not deserve the free mercy of God,"[10] but they do not mention anything in their entire book about the causes that produce this structural poverty, nor about our responsibility regarding those causes.

The exclusivism of some of the affirmations made by their ideological leaders seems to express a God who made a mistake for five hundred years in Latin America, but now has corrected his course and mended his ways by means of this new neo-Calvinist evangelization. For example, Miguel Núñez states, "The movement of the Reformation overlooked Latin America, and this explains why now, five hundred years later, our Latin American nations are experiencing a revival as they understand God's grace for the *very first time*."[11] It gets worse. Don Carson, in the prologue to *Gracia sobre gracia*, seems not to know Latin America when he maintains that "when some people applaud the very rapid growth of evangelicalism in Latin America, they really have not acknowledged that there is very little gospel in its root." He then adds, "There is no sanctification without the power of the word of God and, in my opinion, the Christian legacy that has understood and proclaimed the gospel with the greatest faithfulness and has planted churches that are shaped by the teaching

---

9. Bryan Chapell, "Qué es el Evangelio," in Carson and Keller, *La centralidad del Evangelio*, 154.

10. D. A. Carson and Timothy Keller, "La centralidad del Evangelio en el ministerio," in *La centralidad del Evangelio*, 13.

11. Emphasis added. Miguel Núñez, *El poder de la Palabra para transformar una nación: Un llamado bíblico e histórico a la iglesia latinoamericana* (Medellín: Poiema, 2017), 147.

of Scripture is the legacy of the Protestant Reformation."[12] Therefore, I insist that God has not made a mistake.

It is discouraging to see these declarations and to contrast them with the growth of Christianity that overcame the Guatemalan earthquake in 1976. It also overcame the armed conflict that lasted many years and left thousands dead. The growth of Protestantism also overcame years of military dictatorships, on the right and on the left, in South America and Central America. These statements cause great pain when we think of those Christians who faced the dangers of malaria, dengue, jungles, and mountains, and carried the light of the gospel and of the Scriptures in local languages to remote places. We are convinced of the transforming power of God the Father, who through the Spirit has worked in the proclamation of the gospel of Jesus Christ the length and breadth of our America for so many decades. From what we can see, some of the leaders who have made these affirmations have good intentions and desire to motivate deep study and the preaching of Scripture and to plant healthy churches. Nevertheless, their limited vision of the gospel has led some of them to exaggerate their affirmations and, thereby, project a distorted image of God. God has not made a mistake. He brought salvation and transformation years before these new neighbors reached our lands.

Without a doubt, not everything is negative. There are positive aspects of the image of God that can be redeemed from the writings of this Gospel Coalition movement. God is near and he desires to rescue people from their condition of eternal condemnation. God loves them and desires their repentance. This emphasis will bring some balance to the image of "a good-natured God who is a little naïve" that is spreading in our Latin America. This God will work in favor of humanity.

Conclusions

This small reflection invites us to be conscious of the images of God that circulate in our lands and calls us to evaluate them in light of the teaching of Scripture. If we do this, we will be able to proclaim a more balanced image which is close to the God revealed in the word of God. The image of the angry God is the most frequently seen, although it competes with the God subordinated to humans, or the image of a politically biased God. Each image has a degree of acceptance. This not only affects the common reading and

---

12. D. A. Carson, "Prologue," in *Gracia sobre gracia: La nueva reforma en el mundo hispano*, eds. Juan Sánchez et al. (Medellín: Poiema, 2015), 8–9.

interpretation of the Scriptures, but it also acts like a filter through which the message of the Bible is heard and interpreted. A conscientious teaching and discipleship will seek to correct these distortions in order to bring balance and freedom to the people of God.

This is also a call for humility, respect, and dialogue among the people of God. God the Father did not make a mistake with Latin America. He has spoken and acted in and through his daughters and sons for centuries in our lands. He will continue to do so. Without a doubt, we will need to return, time and again, to the Scriptures, because in them we have eternal life, and they bear witness to the Triune God who brings good news. This truth should not be used as an excuse to divide the people of God, nor to underestimate that the God who brings us salvation will have the last word.

References

Botta, Alejandro F., and Pablo R. Andiñach. *The Bible and the Hermeneutics of Liberation*. Society of Biblical Literature Semeia Studies. Atlanta: Society of Biblical Literature, 2009.

Carson, D. A. "Prologue." In *Gracia sobre gracia: La nueva reforma en el mundo hispano*, edited by Juan Sánchez et al., 7–9. Medellín: Poiema, 2015.

Carson, D. A., and Timothy Keller, eds. *La centralidad del Evangelio*. Miami: Patmos, 2014.

Deiros, Pablo A. *El mundo religioso latinoamericano*. El Paso: Casa Bautista, 2017.

Durán, Juan Guillermo, and Rubén Darío García. "Los coloquios de los 'Doce Apóstoles' de México: Los primeros albores de la predicación evangélica en el Nuevo Mundo." *Revista de la Facultad de Teología de la Pontificia Católica Argentina* 34 (1979): 131–85.

Gehman, James A. "Definición de la misión integral e implicaciones para la hermenéutica bíblica." *Kairós* 45, no. 2 (2009): 109–34.

Núñez, Miguel. *El poder de la Palabra para transformar una nación: Un llamado bíblico e histórico a la iglesia latinoamericana*. Medellín: Poiema, 2017.

Padilla DeBorst, Santiago James. "Decolonial Integral Mission? Development and Contextualization at New Scales." *Journal of Latin American Theology* 13, no. 1 (2018): 65–75.

Sicre, José Luis. "El Dios de los profetas: Contra una imagen 'light' del Dios cristiano." *Sal Terrae* 76 (1988): 419–26.

Villaseñor, Bedolla. "La Teología de la Liberación: Pastoral y violencia revolucionarias." *Revista de Estudios Latinoamericanos* 64 (2017): 185–221.

3

The Gospel in the Haystack

Sadrac Meza

The concept of "gospel" has been key for Christianity from its beginning right up to today. Christianity puts its own identity at risk in its definition of this concept, and this does not apply only to those Christians who call themselves "evangelical." Nevertheless, to search for the gospel in the twenty-first century is like looking for a needle in a haystack. Some people have not realized that there is only one gospel.[1] The haystack of gospels has grown and becomes larger every day (or at least it seems that way). What does this haystack contain? By way of illustration, let's recall the gospel of Roman Empire worship, the gospel of the Judaizers, the gospel of the Gnostics, the gospel of the neo-Platonists, and so on, until we get to the contemporary gospels, whether they be Protestant or Catholic, social or spiritual, liberationist or neo-Pentecostal, modern or postmodern, critical or not critical, and also – why not admit it – Calvinist gospels, Arminian gospels, and so on. Regarding this situation, and showing us a way forward, René Padilla states, "The question that we need to ask ourselves regarding any of the doctrinal formulations that are currently circulating and that claim to be a synthesis of the gospel is not whether they are effective but whether they are the biblical gospel."[2]

---

1. The fact that there are four Gospels (Matthew, Mark, Luke, and John) does not mean that the early church thought that there were four gospels. The very titles that these writings received point to the unity of the gospel: the Gospel according to Matthew, the Gospel according to Mark, etc. In this chapter I use the word "Gospel" (in uppercase) to refer to the writings in the Bible and "gospel" (in lowercase) to refer to the biblical content that is the power of God for salvation to all who believe.

2. C. René Padilla, *Misión Integral: Ensayos sobre el reino y la iglesia* (Buenos Aires: Nueva Creación, 1986), 61.

The Greek word *euangelion* is polysemic, and with the development of Christian doctrine it has become a technical term. In its first use it referred to the message proclaimed by Jesus concerning the kingdom of God. In its second use, the word "gospel" made reference to the message about Jesus proclaimed by the early church, with special emphasis on his death and resurrection. Then, third, "gospel" refers to written documents that narrate the life, work, suffering, death, and resurrection of Jesus Christ (which in this chapter I will always write with an upper case "G": Gospels). Fourth, the concept of gospel is inclusive; it includes what we call the central, essential, or integral message of the Bible. In other words, its etymological meaning of "good news" requires a complex amplification. It is precisely this last sense of the word that we are analyzing in this chapter.

What is the problem: the haystack or the needle? The gospel is a mystery that has been revealed. In the beginning it was a stumbling block for Jews and madness for Greeks. In the second century, Marcion rejected the Old Testament as a witness to the gospel, among other actions.. This anticipated twenty-one centuries of conflicts over interpretation. This is due to the fact that the gospel is both a narrative and an interpretation. Some want and search for an absolute historical and scientific verification, which is not possible. The reason is that the gospel comes to us as an interpretation of the events of the Scriptures that give witness to it. We have been studying Scripture for a long time and it is still difficult to know what the gospel is. The gospel comes from both the Old and New Testaments. We observe that the gospel is woven into the very fabric of biblical history according to the following Pauline formulation:

> Paul, a servant of Christ Jesus, called to be an apostle and set apart for the gospel of God – the gospel he promised beforehand through his prophets in the Holy Scriptures regarding his Son, who as to his earthly life was a descendant of David, and who through the Spirit of holiness was appointed the Son of God in power by his resurrection from the dead: Jesus Christ our Lord. Through him we received grace and apostleship to call all the Gentiles to the obedience that comes from faith for his name's sake. And you also are among those Gentiles who are called to belong to Jesus Christ.
>
> To all in Rome who are loved by God and called to be his holy people:
>
> > Grace and peace to you from God our Father and from the Lord Jesus Christ. (Rom 1:1–7)

The good news (gospel) regarding the search for the gospel is that there seem to be a lot of people interested in this topic today. We need only mention the recent attempts to remember, define, or reformulate the gospel by the Gospel Coalition, or the writings of authors such as Matthew Bates, Scot McKnight, and Jeremy Treat, among others, in the English-speaking world.[3] There is a type of evangelical literature revival regarding this topic. The good news (gospel) has also reached Latin America, although some do not seem to have realized this fact. Although there is only one gospel, and it was given once to the saints, the only way to renew it in the twenty-first century is by believing in the gospel, living the gospel, and preaching the gospel. It is impossible not to have a concept of what the gospel is, whether by embracing it or denying it. False gospels, caricatures of the gospel, rumors of the gospel, and truncated gospels will always be with us. But which one is the true gospel? When does a gospel stop being the gospel?

Formal and Material Criteria to Define the Gospel

Before we try to answer the question directly, we need to say a word about the assumptions regarding the search and its answer. The fact that there are irreconcilable proposals about what the gospel is comes from the fact that there are different assumptions. Other proposals about what the gospel is are different not primarily because the assumptions are different, but rather in the way they are understood and applied. Here is where the topic of what is the gospel is intertwined with the theological question regarding the essence of Christianity. To define the gospel is a theological task. That is, the concept of God, the concept of the Bible, the concept of revelation, the concept of the canon, and so on, have much to say regarding the answer that we will end up with regarding what the gospel is.

The Definition of the Gospel Presupposes the Revelation of God

The gospel presupposes that God exists and that he has communicated with people to tell them about his plan of salvation. This means he has told them what he was doing, what he was going to do, what he has done, and what he will do for the salvation of human beings. God expressed his will for people

---

3. See Matthew W. Bates, *Gospel Allegiance* (Grand Rapids: Brazos, 2019); Scot McKnight, *The King Jesus Gospel: The Original Good News Revisited* (Grand Rapids: Zondervan, 2011); Jeremy R. Treat, *The Crucified King* (Grand Rapids: Zondervan, 2014).

(communication, revelation, salvation) and that has been revealed in Scripture. Therefore, the last word about what is the gospel is contained in the word of God.

The Definition of the Gospel Presupposes a Process of Interpretation

The gospel presupposes that the Scriptures are the word of God in human words (the fullness of language) written through history. The principal theme of the literary work is the history of salvation in Jesus Christ, son of David and son of Abraham. There are no shortcuts for understanding the gospel. A knowledge of Scripture is needed, and this begins with an acknowledgment of its nature, its purpose, and an adequate approach to interpret it.

The Definition of the Gospel Presupposes the Unity of the Message of the Biblical Canon

That is, the definition of the gospel is the result of the hermeneutical process of relating the parts to the whole and the whole to the parts. One or various parts of the Bible, isolated from other passages, do not lead us to the knowledge of the gospel of God. We do not believe that the intention of the Scriptures is to present one gospel in the Old Testament, a different gospel proclaimed by Jesus, and another different gospel announced by the early church. Such approaches do not pay attention to biblical history, nor to the content or the expressed intentions of the biblical authors. It is by paying attention to all that is said, to all the parts, to all its histories, and to all its teachings, that we will understand the central meaning of what the gospel is. The Scriptures being what they are, with their literary, theological, and historical variety, there is no reason to assume that the gospel is completely expressed in just one way. That the Bible has an integral message does not mean that it can be expressed in only one way.

The Definition of the Gospel Should Pay Attention to Its Eschatological Dimension

It is its eschatological dimension that provides and explains the unity of the biblical message. The gospel preached by Jesus during his ministry cannot be identical in all its dimensions to the gospel in the early church, for the simple reason that Jesus had not died or been resurrected. Teachings from the Old Testament cannot be implemented directly in the church for the simple reason that the church, although it is the new Israel, does not exist in the same eschatological moment. By using the phrase "eschatological dimension," we mean to say that the temporal aspect is fundamental for understanding the biblical gospel. In biblical history, the gospel is first promise and then fulfillment. The biblical gospel is dynamic. The gospel has its first days and its last times. In biblical history, the gospel is proclaimed again and again but in different ways. The biblical gospel is a revelation in progress. In other words, the biblical gospel is a story.

The Definition of the Gospel Requires That We Pay Attention First to the Biblical Story and Then to the Later Conceptual Formulations

By "the later conceptual formulations" I am referring to the history of theological reflection. The two tasks are both necessary, but in different ways. It is not possible to express the gospel only in biblical language, although there are examples in the Bible itself of attempts to express the essence of the gospel. But the conceptual formulations that Christian theological reflection has produced down through the ages need to be evaluated by each new generation taking the biblical story as foundational. We cannot attribute absolute value to any historical conceptualization of the gospel.

To Define the Gospel Is a Constant Task for Each Generation of Christians

Padilla reminds us that "all too frequently it is assumed that we Christians already know our message and the only thing we now need is a better strategy and more efficient methods to communicate it."[4] The definition of the gospel requires a process of interpretation of the Scriptures and demands a constant effort by each generation to know it, appropriate it, and proclaim it. The definition of what is the gospel for each generation is needed in order to be faithful to the Lord in our historical context. Let us remember the words of G. Stanton: "The same *gospel* can be said in a different epoch as long as it is said in a different way."[5]

---

4. Padilla, *Misión Integral*, 60.
5. G. Stanton, *Jesús y el Evangelio* (Bilbao: Desclée de Brouwer, 2008), 105.

What Is the Gospel?

The biblical gospel is a christological, soteriological, and deontological gospel. We will use these distinctions with a conceptual purpose. They are to help our understanding of the work of God. These distinctions or dimensions do not mean that they are separate from each other in the gospel. The salvation that the gospel announces is a whole. What God has brought together we should not separate. There is a unity, and, I would add, a unifying thought, that is the fruit of the Spirit: "There is one body and one Spirit, just as you were called to one hope when you were called; one Lord, one faith, one baptism; one God and Father of all, who is over all and through all and in all" (Eph 4:4–6).

Let's remember that we should explain these dimensions of the gospel in light of the criteria and assumptions we outlined in the previous section. You cannot know the gospel that is Jesus Christ without going to the school of God, without going through the divine pedagogy. This pedagogy is the two-thousand-year history between Abraham and Jesus Christ. Abraham, Isaac, Jacob, Joseph, the nation of Israel, and their history: all this constitutes the pedagogy of God. The law is the tutor that guides us to Christ. But it is not only the law that is a tutor. Israel and its history are also a tutor that leads us to Christ.

The Gospel Is Christological

"For God so loved the world that he gave his one and only Son, that whoever believes in him shall not perish but have eternal life" (John 3:16). The christological gospel (the Son) and the soteriological gospel (that they may have eternal life) flow from God's love, from God's grace – so great are this love and grace that existed before the foundation of the world. But the greatness of this love is seen more in the quality of love: God did not hesitate (shrink back) from giving his one and only Son. "God's grace – as Paul taught – is infinitely greater than human sin or even the divine reaction to that sin."[6]

The gospel does not begin with the announcement of salvation (the soteriological dimension). The gospel begins with the announcement of the Savior. What other conclusion can be reached from the two-thousand-year history that prepared the Savior (Matt 1:1–17)? I am referring to the biblical history between Abraham and Jesus ("Jesus the Messiah the son of David, the son of Abraham"). What other purpose identified Israel and the law, except the preparation for the coming of the Savior ("When the set time had fully

---

6. A. Ganoczy, *De su plenitud todos hemos recibido* (Barcelona: Herder, 1991), 38.

come, God sent his Son, born of a woman, born under the law," Gal 4:4)? Israel and all its institutions would prefigure the identity of the Savior (and, of course, of salvation, because, as we recall, we can separate these two dimensions only conceptually).

Salvation cannot be separated from the Savior. In addition, "I will be your God," "I will be with you," and "God with us" are the most common formulations of God's promise in the Bible. There is nothing that so clearly shows God's initiative in salvation as these formulations.

This dimension of a personal relationship between the holy God and his people is precisely what the forgiveness of sins and the gift of the Holy Spirit demand. In other words, the christological aspect demands the other two – the soteriological and the deontological dimensions of the gospel. But the deontological dimension makes the soteriological dimension possible. The relationship as children of God, which is communicated in the blessing of Matthew 5:9, is possible only through the forgiveness of sins and the gift of the Holy Spirit. And holiness, without which no one will see the Lord, is made reality by the Holy Spirit (soteriology). That holiness is for this life, and what is not obtainable in this life will be obtained in the next life.

The gospel of the kingdom of God cannot be separated from the King. The Messiah of God reigns. In this suffering Messiah, God rescues and transports human beings from darkness to the kingdom of his beloved Son. No longer slaves to sin, now they are servants/slaves of justice. Slavery to justice is paradoxically called freedom, the freedom of the children of God.

The gospel begins to become known when people start to know the identity of the Savior ("you are to give him the name Jesus, because he will save his people from their sins," Matt 1:21). The identity of the Savior says a lot about the need or problem of humanity. Who is the Savior? He is the seed of Abraham, the prophet like Moses, the King, Son of David, the Messiah, the Christ, the Son of God, the Son of Man, the Word, the Suffering Servant of Yahweh, God, the Lord, the great High Priest.[7] This multifaceted identity of the person who is the gospel (that is why we mention the christological dimension) has testimony by the privileged witnesses of the gospel, namely the Scriptures of the Old Testament and the Scriptures of the New Testament.[8] This is why we affirm that the gospel cannot be separated from the Jesus of history,[9] but we

---

7. O. Cullman, *Cristología del Nuevo Testamento* (Salamanca: Sígueme, 1998).

8. John R. W. Stott, *La misión cristiana hoy* (Buenos Aires: Certeza, 1977).

9. F. F. Bruce, "When Is a Gospel Not a Gospel?," *Bulletin of the John Rylands Library* 45, no. 2 (1963): 319–39.

should be quick to say that we are referring to the biblical history (Matt 1:1–17) and not to an untrustworthy human reconstruction that does not even respect the biblical sources.

As a specific example, we cite the preaching of the gospel by Peter in Acts 2. After explaining the coming of the Holy Spirit as the fulfillment of the Scriptures of the Old Testament, Peter focuses his sermon on Jesus of Nazareth, his death and resurrection, to reach the climax of his conclusion: "Therefore let all Israel be assured of this: God has made this Jesus, whom you crucified, both Lord and Messiah" (Acts 2:36). The biblical gospel contains two basic affirmations: Jesus Christ is Lord, and Jesus Christ is the Savior.[10]

That the gospel is christological means that salvation is not a gift separated from the Savior. The gospel is an invitation to receive the forgiveness of sins and the gift of the Holy Spirit from the Savior who is Lord, Messiah, and King ("Exalted to the right hand of God, he has received from the Father the promised Holy Spirit and has poured out what you now see and hear," Acts 2:33). Salvation comes from the Savior to human beings so that humanity may come back to the Savior. The gospel is an invitation to accept the reconciliation with God in Christ. To receive the gospel is not to add a good luck amulet, nor to have an ace up one's sleeve, nor to win the lottery. To receive the gospel is to receive our adoption as children. To receive the gospel is to receive a hope for the future and a reality for the present. It is to enter into a new present reality, the reality of the knowledge of God, the reality of friendship with God, the reality of being part of the family of God, the reality of living in the Spirit, the reality of entering the kingdom of God. The gospel is the good news that we are invited by the King to become part of his family and of his kingdom. We are invited to enter the kingdom of God through faith in the Savior.

The Gospel Is Soteriological

It is impossible to speak of Christology without speaking of soteriology (as noted in the previous section). The personal name of the Christ is Savior (Jesus). Biblical history speaks of the second person of the Trinity (the Son), but not to reveal the Son in isolation. Biblical history, when it wants to speak of salvation, has to speak of the Savior (the Son of God). What is most important is to recognize that salvation, the soteriological dimension of the gospel, is based on what Jesus did and not on what any other human being could do. It is not that humans saw that they had a problem and were looking for a savior.

---

10. Stott, *La misión cristiana hoy.*

No. In fact, it was just the opposite. Most of the time, people do not even realize that they are lost, in need of a savior. Therefore, salvation cannot be separated from the Savior and what he does.

Although we could provide an interpretation regarding the needs of people today and use relevant language, this is not what should guide us in our understanding of what salvation is. Salvation should be defined not only biblically but also christologically: Who Jesus is (the christological dimension of the gospel), and what Jesus did (the soteriological dimension of the gospel). The need for salvation is to be defined and understood by what the Savior did. That is why only in theory can we distinguish the christological dimension in the gospel from its soteriological dimension.

The new covenant promised (Jer 31; Ezek 36) and fulfilled in Jesus has two pillars: the forgiveness of sins and the gift of the Holy Spirit. The first was realized by the Savior in his death and resurrection; and the second, in the pouring out of the Holy Spirit when he was enthroned and seated at the right hand of God. Therefore, the apostle Paul teaches us that two events in the life of the Savior are crucial for understanding salvation (1 Cor 15:1–11). The first is the death of our Lord Jesus Christ according to the Scriptures, and the second, the resurrection of our Lord according to the Scriptures. We should note that the death of Jesus Christ for us is not only an event in the New Testament. Neither is it an event that was prepared only since the time of Abraham. It had been prepared since the time of Adam and Eve. It is an event that acquires its own identity in the ceremonial law of Moses, as the letter to the Hebrews explains. Jesus Christ died for our sins. Jesus Christ rose from the dead so that the entirety of humanity could also be resurrected, spiritually in this life and bodily for eternal life.

Knowing what the Savior did, we can now clearly understand what humanity's need is. People are sinners by nature. Human sin brings with it guilt and corruption. The entire physical creation and society show the consequences of human sin. It is for this reason that salvation has the two pillars of the forgiveness of sins and the gift of the Holy Spirit. The forgiveness of sins takes away the guilt and removes the condemnation. But what about the corruption of human nature? The Savior gives the gift of and baptism with the Holy Spirit which transforms humans and forms the image of Christ in his brothers and sisters. With the forgiveness of sins and the gift of the Holy Spirit, the Savior creates a new person, a new humanity, a new creation. God and his people, the people of God and God, living in peace. "The what of the gospel determines the how its effects are implemented in practical life."[11]

Another way we see the indivisible relationship between Savior and salvation is in the fact that the Savior took it upon himself to live a human life. This is not something merely additional. At the very least, we can affirm that his life is an example or model that he gives and desires for his followers. He took time to teach his disciples how to live (Mark 3–10). Be imitators of me as I am of Christ, said the apostle Paul.

Although salvation history necessarily implies that it is directed toward people who need salvation, the biblical gospel begins with the surprising news that it is God who is reconciling people to himself. Those who were not seeking God received salvation. This radically changes the emphasis. The salvation announced by the gospel can never take as its center the human being, or human needs, or human initiative. Mark 1:14 states that Jesus preached the gospel of God. Therefore, although the gospel is for humanity, it was born out of the free love of God (John 3:16).

The Deontological Gospel

In a (biblical) sense, the first Christian was Abraham. That is why he is called the father of all believers, whether Jews or Gentiles. What did God give to Abraham? His love, his revelation, his friendship, his promise, and so on. All this is true. But, in fact, the very first thing that God gave to Abraham was a command:

> Go from your country, your people and your father's household
> to the land I will show you.
>
> > I will make you into a great nation,
> >   and I will bless you;
> > I will make your name great,
> >   and you will be a blessing.
> > I will bless those who bless you,
> >   and whoever curses you I will curse;
> > and all peoples on earth
> >   will be blessed through you. (Gen 12:1–3)

From the phrase "I will make you," all that follows is what God will do (I will make you into a great nation, I will bless you, I will make your name great,

---

11. Padilla, *Misión integral*, 60.

etc.). But God cannot do the first thing. Leaving his country and his father's household is something that Abraham has to do. Obviously God could have forced Abraham to leave his country, but this would not be called faith nor obedience. Abraham's response is what the Bible calls Abraham's faith.

Someone might say that Abraham's faith refers to his belief that God would give him a son and descendants, based on a reading of Genesis 15:1-6. I would completely agree. But it was not only this. It also meant that Abraham believed that God would provide a land, that his descendants would be numerous, that God would bless him, and that his descendants would become a means of salvation for all nations. But let us remember that all of these promises had been announced in Genesis 12 and that Abraham's obedience included them. Abraham is the father of faith because his was obedience and not merely acknowledgment or assent (Jas 2:21-23).

Just as Abraham had a specific command to obey in order to begin his friendship with God, the gospel similarly has a specific command for people to receive salvation. Let's look at some examples from Scripture: "The time has come. . . . The kingdom of God has come near. Repent and believe the good news" (Mark 1:15). We have already alluded to Peter's sermon in Acts 2:38 where he says, "Repent and be baptized, every one of you, in the name of Jesus Christ for the forgiveness of your sins. And you will receive the gift of the Holy Spirit." Paul and Silas tell the Philippian jailer in Acts 16:31: "Believe in the Lord Jesus, and you will be saved – you and your household." And in Acts 17:30, while preaching in Athens, Paul warns that "in the past God overlooked [people's] ignorance, but now he commands all people everywhere to repent." Romans 10:9-10 is another pertinent passage: "If you declare with your mouth, 'Jesus is Lord,' and believe in your heart that God raised him from the dead, you will be saved. For it is with your heart that you believe and are justified, and it is with your mouth that you profess your faith and are saved."

The command of the gospel is conversion. As the best theologies clarify, conversion includes repentance and faith or belief in the gospel. The repentance that God requires is a repentance that acknowledges that we have sinned against God, that we deserve God's punishment, and that we are not worthy. The parable of the prodigal son in Luke 15 is a good example: "Father, I have sinned against heaven and against you. I am no longer worthy to be called your son; make me like one of your hired servants" (Luke 15:18-19).

Faith is the interior attitude (acknowledgment, will [decision], feelings, motives, reasons, purposes) that appropriates the message of the gospel. It begins with a knowledge of the gospel. Obviously, it is a knowledge of the christological and soteriological gospel. As a consequence, the proclamation of the gospel is very important, because it is the power of God for salvation to everyone who believes. "How, then, can they call on the one they have not believed in? And how can they believe in the one of whom they have not heard? And how can they hear without someone preaching to them? And how can anyone preach unless they are sent?" (Rom 10:14–15a).

Faith continues with trust placed in the gospel. What the Scriptures affirm about the Savior (the christological gospel) and about salvation (the soteriological gospel) is appropriated as truth by the believer. It is appropriated as the most important object in the world. It is appropriated as something one is willing to live for or die for. The gospel is the pearl of great price. The gospel is the treasure found in a field. Jesus Christ is the way, the truth, and the life. There is no other name under heaven by which we can be saved. God is in Christ reconciling the world to himself. Only Jesus has words of eternal life. To believe is to trust in the veracity of these affirmations.

Faith continues with the public confession spoken of in Romans 10 or with the baptism in water mentioned by Peter in Acts 2. It is a public confession. Faith is a process that has a beginning but not an end. It is entering through the narrow gate and walking along the narrow way (Christians were first known as those of "the way").

It is important to clarify that the deontological dimension of the gospel does not refer to that which is commonly called discipleship or sanctification. The process of transformation, the process of sanctification, is essential to the gospel and the Christian life (the soteriological dimension). In other words, it is part of the content of the proclaimed gospel. As such, it is the object of the believer's faith. The unbeliever, upon hearing the gospel, is converted in order to receive the forgiveness of sins and the gift of the Holy Spirit who implements the process of sanctification. The command of the gospel (the deontological dimension) is to repent and to believe in the gospel (to believe in the Savior and in his salvation).

Conclusion

The question regarding the essence of the gospel is a theological question. In addition, it is tightly connected to the question regarding the essence of Christianity. As we observe the content of the literature on this topic, I consider it better to understand the question regarding the essence of Christianity and the question about the essence of the gospel as more specific, although both fall within the field of theology. The manner in which we address the question regarding the gospel is conditioned by assumptions derived from the answer to the question, "What is the essence of Christianity?"

Every definition of the biblical gospel is an interpretation and an effort at synthesis. It should be evaluated by Christians using the criteria of biblical revelation. The fact that these efforts are not perfect does not reduce their value and importance. But we must also acknowledge that there are revisionist interpretations of the gospel, such as that proposed by Borg,[12] who speaks of a new paradigm of Christianity which, in my opinion, is totally misguided.

Although there is no perfect and complete definition of what the gospel is, we must be aware that there are "gospels" that are not the gospel. For example, in the first place, a gospel separated from biblical history is not the gospel. A gospel based exclusively on the New Testament is not the gospel. Neither is a gospel based exclusively on the four Gospels. Second, a gospel that does not give appropriate emphasis to the sufferings, death, and resurrection (and ascension) of Jesus Christ is not the gospel. Third, a gospel that does not acknowledge the difference between Creator and creature, between the holy God and sinful humans, between the Savior Jesus Christ and those in need of salvation, is not the gospel. Fourth, a gospel that adds conditions that go beyond the conversion (repentance and faith) of human beings is not the gospel. And fifth, a gospel that does not include the transformation of human beings is not the biblical gospel. Although people can experience conversion just before they die (like the thief who was crucified next to Jesus), God's plan for the overwhelming majority is that they live out their lives as the salt of the earth and the light of the world.

References

Bates, Matthew W. *Gospel Allegiance*. Grand Rapids: Brazos, 2019.
Borg, Marcus J. *The Heart of Christianity: Rediscovering a Life of Faith*. New York: HarperOne, 2003.
Bruce, F. F. "When Is a Gospel Not a Gospel?" *Bulletin of the John Rylands Library* 45, no. 2 (1963): 319–39.
Cullman, O. *Cristología del Nuevo Testamento*. Salamanca: Sígueme, 1998.
Ganoczy, A. *De su plenitud todos hemos recibido*. Barcelona: Herder, 1991.
McKnight, Scot. *The King Jesus Gospel: The Original Good News Revisited*. Grand Rapids: Zondervan, 2011.

---

12. Marcus J. Borg, *The Heart of Christianity: Rediscovering a Life of Faith* (New York: HarperOne, 2003).

Padilla, C. René. *Misión Integral: Ensayos sobre el reino y la iglesia*. Buenos Aires: Nueva Creación, 1986.
Stanton, G. *Jesús y el Evangelio*. Bilbao: Desclée de Brouwer, 2008.
Stott, John R. W. *La misión cristiana hoy*. Buenos Aires: Certeza, 1977.
Treat, Jeremy R. *The Crucified King*. Grand Rapids: Zondervan, 2014.

4

The Bible, Female Leadership, and Latin American Hermeneutics

Javier Ortega Badilla

Theological reflection in Latin America is determined by the conviction that everything related to human ideas, including theological ideas, is connected to the present from where those ideas emerged. Therefore, Latin American theologians are challenged to develop their discipline in a rigorous dialogue between those "disciplines that open up the past and those disciplines that explain the present" with a methodology that has been defined as "the continuous change in our interpretation of the Bible as a function of the continuous changes in our present reality."[1]

We are interested here in reflecting on a particular use of the Bible that opposes the leadership of women in the church. This is an interpretation that, according to our understanding, consciously or unconsciously ignores decades of sound biblical reflection in Latin America. It has opted for readings that know very little about the dialogue that exists with disciplines that are open to the past or explain the present.

There are two passages that are central to the discussion and will serve as examples of this misinterpretation: 1 Corinthians 11:2–16 and 14:34–37.

---

1. Juan Luis Segundo, *Liberación de la Teología*, Cuadernos Latinoamericanos (Buenos Aires: Carlo Lohle, 1975), 12.

The Use of the Bible That Opposes Female Leadership
The Man Is Head of the Woman (1 Cor 11:2–16)

For those sectors that oppose female leadership in the church, this biblical passage shows the subordination of women to men in our day. It is true that the text speaks about the manner in which women should wear their hair in public worship. This, as we shall see later on, was very important in the Greco-Roman culture of the first century after Christ. But it is also true that, to bolster this teaching, Paul refers to an argument in which the way a woman wears her hair would be a visible sign of subordination understood by everyone; to wear your hair in a different way would imply going against nature and accepted custom. In essence, the way a woman wore her hair would be nothing other than the visible expression of the established hierarchy between men and women. Based on this reading, a current application is suggested: "Men's hair should be short, and he should not cover his head (with a hat), while women's hair should be long, as a visible acknowledgment of her submission to God's order. She should wear a veil, not to cover her face (as Muslim women do), but to cover the rest of her head."[2]

Culver, whom we are quoting here, laments that the topic of women wearing long hair or a hat or veil has largely been forgotten. It seems inconsistent to him that women attend all kinds of public meetings without covering their heads.[3] The woman should cover her head because the man has authority over her, while the man should not cover his head because no authority is over him except Jesus.

Those who oppose female leadership raise Paul's use of the creation narrative to the level of an archetype. They say that the elements highlighted by Paul are and should be highlighted at all times and in every culture: (1) Woman is derived from man, independently from the next phrase that man proceeds from woman; (2) woman was created because of man and not vice versa.[4]

Therefore, the only way to affirm that the subordination of woman to man is a transcultural element and, therefore, applicable at all times is to deny the cultural character of the elements in the passage under analysis: the interpretation of creation, the conception of nature, the understanding of

---

2. Robert D. Culver, "Una postura tradicionalista: 'Las mujeres guarden silencio,'" in *Mujeres en el Ministerio*, eds. Bonnidell Clouse and Robert G. Clouse (Barcelona: CLIE, 2005), 34. We notice that the order that Paul attributes to nature is attributed here directly to God. We frequently see the use of this interpretation mechanism.

3. Culver, "Una postura tradicionalista," 34.

4. Culver, 37.

shame and honor, and, finally, the use of the veil. An example of this type of argument is found in Foh:

> To relativize the biblical commands for women, they [those in favor of female leadership] have utilized a hermeneutical principle that consists in considering the historical, cultural, and geographical context.... Nevertheless, to be aware of the culture and customs of an era should not relativize the command. God chose the moment and the era to reveal that command, and God is not limited either by time or by space. The only thing that could possibly suggest a temporal or limited character of the text would be some concrete indication that appeared in the text itself.[5]

One could imagine that if God chose "the moment and the era," he would also have taken into account the culture of "the moment and the era," because if he had not, his communication would have been incomprehensible. Therefore, Foh's argument above turns God's revelation into something absolutely atemporal, ahistorical, and, as a result, incomprehensible.

The application of this interpretation to our current day has obvious consequences for female leadership in the church. If such leadership implies authority over those one is supposed to guide, then of course this authority cannot be given to a woman, because the Bible teaches that a woman should be subordinate to a man, which is expressed by her wearing something visible over her hair when she participates in the worship service. Foh points out:

> 1 Corinthians 11:2–16 teaches that women can and should actively participate in the worship, by praying and prophesying. The only requirement is that they cover their heads so that the glory will go to God and not to their husbands; this requirement is necessary because a woman's husband is the head.[6]

As we will see later on, an interpretation like the one we have just presented is imaginable only if we refuse to explore the biblical text from other possible angles. Such a refusal, consciously or unconsciously, serves functionally as a way to treat women unjustly. This treatment springs from a conception of gender that a growing number of Christians intuitively know is unjust, although they do not have the technical tools to denounce it as such.

---

5. Susan T. Foh, "Una postura en pro del liderazgo masculino, 'La cabeza de la mujer es el hombre,'" in *Mujeres en el ministerio*, eds. Bonnidell Clouse and Robert G. Clouse (Barcelona: CLIE, 2005), 70.

6. Foh, "Una postura en pro del liderazgo masculino," 89–90.

Let the Women Be Silent in the Church (1 Cor 14:34–37)

It is not difficult to perceive the usefulness that this biblical passage has for those who oppose female leadership in the church. If women cannot talk, how can they exercise any leadership? And especially, how can they serve in any leadership positions such as the pastorate or teach in the church?

It has been correctly noted that the Greek word used to characterize this silence is Σιγαω (*sigaō*), which simply means "not to speak." The prohibition, as our text clarifies, would impede an interruption by women in a service open to debate.[7] But at the same time, they affirm, the text reflects the goodness of Christianity by permitting women to learn at home (v. 35): "When Paul says that women should ask questions at home, he is offering them a space to learn; we see that Paul is not denying education to women. It is important that women learn, but they should not take part in the official teaching of the Church."[8]

The incorporation of sciences that open up the past and explain the present would have shown that silence in the assembly and learning at home were not a Christian novelty. This would have moved us to look for a message for our times that goes beyond a superficial reading.

The Bible as Good News from Latin America

For Latin American theology, obedience to the call of Jesus Christ leads to many new theological developments. That is, first you follow Christ, intuitively, then you make theology as you walk in the way. It is in this intuitive obedience one can perceive, but one almost does not dare to say, that there are certain postures regarding women that do not align with the Jesus who goes ahead of us along the way. Suspicions arise that, on occasion, biblical texts are used with a spirit contrary to that of Jesus. Isn't this what we see when some teachers of the law approached Jesus, quoting Moses regarding an adulterous woman? They found out that Jesus was not willing to submit to a written norm (John 8).

The expression "the Bible says" sounds spiritual and intimidating. Those who use it know quite well that it will provoke this impression in their audience. Not only Pharisees in the time of Jesus, but also some well-known

---

7. Culver, "Una postura tradicionalista," 40.

8. Foh, "Una postura en pro del liderazgo masculino." For a defense of the positive dimension that permits a woman to learn, see Adam Hensley, "Σιγαω, Λαλεω, and ὑποτασσω in 1 Corinthians 14:34 in Their Literary and Rhetorical Context," *Journal of the Evangelical Theological Society* 55, no. 2 (2012): 360.

contemporary preachers use this coercive mechanism. John MacArthur, and others like him, is an example of this:

> In today's church, as in Ephesus, some women are dissatisfied with their God-given roles. They want prominent positions, including opportunities to exercise authority over men. There is only one biblical way to handle those situations for the good of everyone concerned, and that is to do what Paul did. He directly forbade women from taking the authoritative pastor-teacher roles in the church.[9]

This Latin American church will no longer remain silent when expressions like "the Bible says" are misused. If the truth be told, this is not the first time that the church has resolved to follow a path of obedience which goes against what "the Bible says." As an example, we see the position of the majority of Protestant churches regarding slavery or the rape of women. Although the Bible clearly commands slaves to render service to their masters as to the Lord (Eph 6:5),[10] there are very few Protestant Christians who would insist that this is what a slave should do today. Something similar can be said about the delicate topic of rape. We should expect an absolute rejection of such a horrific practice. No Christian in his or her right mind would even consider suggesting that rape victims should claim it was their right to marry their rapists. Even though this seems strange to our ears, this is what a believer who wants to practice biblical teaching will find in what the Bible literally says (Deut 22:28–29).[11]

It is certain that those who oppose female leadership in the church seem not to have fulfilled the task of interpreting the Bible. In fact, they have followed the style and example of the Pharisees in the time of Jesus, who only quoted texts hoping that the Lord himself would submit to them. But today, just as then, following Jesus leads to new and renewing possibilities in the very texts where others find only slavery.

---

9. John MacArthur, "Can Women Exercise Authority in the Church?," Grace to You, 29 August 2013, https://www.gty.org/library/blog/B130829/can-women-exercise-authority-in-the-church.

10. "Slaves, obey your earthly masters with respect and fear, and with sincerity of heart, just as you would obey Christ" (Eph 6:5).

11. "If a man happens to meet a virgin who is not pledged to be married and rapes her and they are discovered, he shall pay her father fifty shekels of silver. He must marry the young woman, for he has violated her. He can never divorce her as long as he lives" (Deut 22:28–29).

An Exegetical and Contextual Analysis of 1 Corinthians 11:2–16

The passage that concerns us belongs to a much longer text. The passage cannot be separated from this longer text if we are going to correctly understand it. Chapters 7 through 14 in 1 Corinthians constitute Paul's answers to a series of questions that had been written to him. These answers deal with domestic issues regarding personal items and congregational daily living. In fact, if there is a general thread in Pauline literature, it is that they are writings that emerge from the concrete needs of the churches. The apostle has already given instructions regarding marriage, divorce, and remarriage (ch. 7). He has also sent his recommendations about what to do with food that had been offered in sacrifice to idols which Corinthian Christians could easily obtain (ch. 8). He explains that the knowledge that some believers have, the truth that idols are not really anything, does not permit them to assume superiority over or to be condescending toward their weaker brothers or sisters whose fragile consciences would be damaged if they saw them eating this food (8:10). The best example would be, according to chapter 9, the apostle himself, who although he recognizes certain rights of every apostle, prefers to deny himself the use of these rights, by becoming weak to the weak (9:22). His instruction, therefore, is that the Corinthians should acquire sufficient maturity to be able to discern what is helpful more than what is permitted (10:23). They are to do this so as not to be a stumbling block either to the Jews or to the Gentiles (10:32), just as Paul aimed to please all, not seeking his own benefit, but the well-being of the many (10:33).

Within this context of these domestic recommendations comes the topic of the attire of women in Christian meetings or worship services (ch. 11). Paul does not want them to be a stumbling block to Jews or Gentiles, but to live in such a way that all might be saved. We need to remember that the goal is not to be a stumbling block to Jews or Gentiles. This is the message.

First, we have a very clear expression of an apparent hierarchical structure presented by Paul. Christ is the head of every man > man is the head of every woman > and God is the head of Christ (11:3). This passage has been greatly debated given that a plain reading seems to clearly defend the subordination of the Son to the Father. We cannot enter this debate in detail here, but we can affirm that there is no doubt about the hierarchical nature of Paul's expression, given that he is using it as the supreme example of the relationship between men and women. Above all, what is under discussion is not Christology, but the appropriate attire to be worn in a public gathering of the church in order not to be a stumbling block to Jews or Gentiles.

The man who covers his head when he prays or prophesies dishonors his own head (11:4). The woman who prays or prophesies with her head uncovered (*akatakaluptos*) likewise dishonors her own head,[12] because having her head uncovered while praying or prophesying is the same as shaving her head (*xuraō*) (11:5).

For the reader from the twenty-first century, it is difficult to understand what might be dishonoring about having one's head shaved. From the perspective of a reasonable exegesis, the only way to explain this is that in Paul's day, this was a convention accepted by all. In effect, given the way Paul makes his argument, we can assume that he knows that his readers agree with him that these denounced elements are, in fact, shameful. Therefore, Paul can point out, with all naturalness, that not covering one's head is just as shameful as cutting one's hair (11:6).

Female and male readers alike would affirm that Paul always, unfailingly, provides some instruction regarding women's behavior. Is Paul obsessed? No. Is Paul a misogynist? No. Given that honor was the most basic social structure category of the first-century Mediterranean world, honor appears when these three elements come together: (1) power, (2) status based on gender, and (3) religion.[13] Regarding gender, honor depended on whether the role assigned by society to both genders was completely fulfilled. This is the reason why Paul was concerned that within the church the roles assigned to women by first-century Mediterranean society should not be altered.[14]

In the first century AD, a woman who did not dress in conformity to the role society assigned to her or did not wear her hair as society expected as a sign of authority, brought dishonor to her husband. And her husband was her head, just as God was the head of Christ. Within the context of the church, this would be a stumbling block to both Jews and Gentiles. This hierarchy is demonstrated by two resources: one written and one natural. On the one hand,

---

12. The word *akatakaluptos*, which is frequently translated as "uncovered," is also used in the LXX in Lev 13:45, where it translates the Hebrew word *para* that means "uncombed" or "hair loosened." We find the same Hebrew expression in Num 5:18 where it refers to a woman who loosens her hair. Remembering that Greek women used ribbons and ornamental combs, some scholars have interpreted that "dishonoring her head" refers to the woman who loosens her hair by not using braids or ribbons that would permit her to tie it to her head: Alan Padgett, "Paul on Women in the Church: The Contradictions of Coiffure in 1 Corinthians 11:2–16," *Journal for the Study of the New Testament* 6, no. 20 (1984): 70.

13. Bruce J. Malina, *El mundo del Nuevo Testamento: Perspectivas desde la antropología cultural*, Agora 1 (Estella: Verbo Divino, 1995), 48–49.

14. To go deeper into the anthropological and cultural studies applied to the Bible, see Bruce J. Malina, *El mundo social de Jesús y los evangelios: La antropología cultural mediterránea y el Nuevo Testamento*, Presencia Teológica 116 (Santander: Sal Terrae, 2002).

the apostle refers to creation to back up his argument: woman came from man and not vice versa (11:8), and woman was created for man and not the opposite (11:9). This way of understanding creation, shared by much of first-century Judaism, was so widespread and accepted that it would be impossible for a woman of that era to rise up and not wear a sign of authority on her head (11:10). It is wrong to think that Paul is introducing for the first time the topic of man's authority over woman, as if it were a Christian novelty. In fact, what he is doing is utilizing a well-known and socially accepted idea to reinforce the tradition of Christian women's attire so that they would not end up becoming a stumbling block to Jews or Gentiles.

The second element that serves Paul's argument is the example of nature (11:13–16). Just as with the example of creation, the apostle assumes that there is a consensus among his readers that permits him to express himself as he does in verse 13: "Judge for yourselves: Is it proper for a woman to pray to God with her head uncovered?" The apostle presupposes that they all know that nature teaches it is dishonorable for a man to let his hair grow long (11:14). Paul shares with his contemporaries a certain understanding of nature, which explains why he doesn't get distracted in explaining what aspect of creation he is referring to or in which aspect of creation he finds a model of what is dishonorable.[15] Neither does he explain what "dishonorable" means, which shows that there is a common understanding between him and his readers. In the same line of reasoning, Paul also supposes that his readers have the knowledge that it is honorable for women to have long hair (11:15). This would surely mean a lot to people in the first century AD, but it is difficult for us to understand today.

As can be seen, there is much in the passage that is not new Christian doctrine. Instead, it is already part of the culture that the apostle shares with his audience: the importance attributed to shame and honor, the concept of what nature teaches regarding the length of one's hair, and the subordination of women to men understood from the interpretation of the creation story.[16] What is new is Paul's insistence that the believers should avoid becoming a stumbling block (10:31–33), because being contentious is not an acceptable practice among the churches of God (11:16). This, as we shall see, is the message of this entire section of 1 Corinthians.

---

15. Some think that wearing one's hair long is related to homosexuality: J. Murphy-O'Connor, "1 Corinthians 11:2–16 Once Again," *The Catholic Biblical Quarterly* 50, no. 2 (1988): 268.

16. We will return to the topic of creation later on, when we analyze 1 Corinthians 14.

Knowing these historical and cultural elements is essential to understanding and applying a biblical passage today. But this supposes an additional effort for honest interpreters of the Bible, that is, to discern if together with the message of the word of God we should also impose cultural elements from the first century.

An Exegetical and Contextual Analysis of 1 Corinthians 14:34–37

In the text of 1 Corinthians 14, Paul continues giving an answer to internal matters related to the gatherings of the Corinthian Christians. In the second half of chapter 11, he introduces the topic of the abuses in the services when they celebrated the Lord's Supper. He then continues with instructions about the appropriate exercise of the gifts of the Spirit (ch. 12), which should also have love as the governing criterion (ch. 13). These are instructions given for the optimal participation in the context of a worship service of a church comprised of Jews and Gentiles, but founded in the heart of a city like Corinth in a time that Paul understood to be the last days. In fact, Paul has already made mention of this by stating that "the time is short" (7:29). Under these conditions, and continuing what we mentioned regarding the passage in 1 Corinthians 11, the behavior of the Corinthians should be carefully measured by the will of God, but also considering the context of the entire city. This is made evident when Paul compares the behavior of the Corinthian Christians with that of the Gentiles to highlight that the Corinthians' sin is worse (5:1), and when he asks whether there aren't people sufficiently wise within the church as there are outside to resolve litigations among believers (ch. 6). All of these issues brought dishonor to the church within the Corinthian context. The writers of the New Testament were very concerned about this disgrace (compare, among other passages, 1 Tim 3:7; 1 Pet 4:15–16).

Chapter 14 continues with the theme of spiritual gifts in which he emphasizes speaking in tongues and prophecy. In this context, the apostle provides, as earlier, specific instructions for women; an issue of honor, as we mentioned earlier. Bruce Malina has pointed out, precisely, that women play an essential role in protecting the honor of a natural group such as the family or the church. We are dealing with the moral division of tasks or "gender-based roles." Not fulfilling one's role would significantly damage the group's honor;[17] this is why Paul is so concerned to provide specific instructions regarding women's conduct.

---

17. Malina, *El mundo del Nuevo Testamento*, 68.

In our text, the apostle is pointing out that the woman should maintain silence in the church (*ekklesia*) because she is not permitted to speak (*epitrepetai*) (14:34). It is interesting that the verb that we translate as "is not permitted" is in the passive voice (from *epitrepo*), from which we can deduce that this is not an original instruction from Paul but an existing norm, known by him and by the original recipients of his letter. In effect, according to Paul, he is pointing out the same rule (*kai ho nomos legei*) that the woman should be in submission (*hypotasso*).[18]

What "law" is Paul talking about? At first glance, it seems that Paul is referring to a Jewish law, which is very strange if he is trying to back up a norm of conduct in a Christian worship service. It is strange in two ways. In the first place, Paul considers Jewish law to be a "wet nurse" needed only until the appointed time was fulfilled, and this has now taken place with the coming of Christ (Gal 3:24–27).

In the second place, Paul is organizing the church by following the model not of the Old Testament, but rather that of the synagogue. Those who suppose that Paul is here referring to the Jewish law of the Old Testament will find it extremely difficult to equate the silence in the *ekklesia* with the silence in the temple. It is much more reasonable to think that Paul is referring to the Greco-Roman law in which women were not allowed to speak in public assemblies, which were called *ekklesia*. In the normal practice of the period, women "did not even attend the public assembly (*ekklesia*), which was the most important institution of political decision-making, together with the magistrates. In effect, women could not vote or speak."[19] We should not consider it strange that Paul appeals to a common custom (or rule or law). Paul is a citizen of his time who is seeking the best way for the church to carry out its mission without unnecessary problems and without causing others to stumble.

If the woman wants to learn, she should ask her husband at home, because it is disgraceful (*aischros*) for her to speak in the church (*ekklesia*) (v. 35). It is possible that the message of the gospel had led the Corinthian women to believe that these customs had changed within the *ekklesia* of God. But Paul, given the conditions of the city and of the times in which they were living, has to make sure that things are done "in a fitting and orderly way" according

---

18. The verb *hypotasso*, which we translate as being in submission or subordination in v. 34, is the same verb that is used in Rom 13:1, where everyone is to be in submission to those in authority. This means that here we are talking about a hierarchical submission just as the male-female relationship was understood in the first century AD.

19. E. W. Stegemann and W. Stegemann, *Historia social del cristianismo primitivo: Los inicios en el judaísmo y las comunidades cristianas*, Agora 8 (Estella: Verbo Divino, 2008), 494.

to the customs of the time (1 Cor 14:40). There is a text from a few centuries prior to Paul – but influential in the formation of the cultural values of the period – which illustrates well how a woman understood her role in society. This is a portion of Aristophanes' *Lysistrata*:

> For a long time, we suffered in silence; because we knew our place, we let you do just anything you wanted. You didn't even let us grumble – and we didn't like it! We saw right through you, and often we found out that you had made a bad decision about something important. Although we were hurting inside, we asked you with a smile; "In the assembly today, what did you do about the peace treaty?" "Mind your own business!" said my husband. "Keep quiet." So I did.
>
> So then we heard you'd passed an even worse decree, and I would ask, "Dear husband, why do you persist in such a stupid policy?" He'd give me a nasty look, and say if I did not get on with spinning, he'd give me a headache. "War is men's business!"[20]

That the woman keep silent in the church and that she learn by asking her husband at home was not a new idea that originated with Christianity. It corresponds to what was considered "fitting and orderly" according to the customs of the times (14:40). Curiously, this is what is revealed in the instructions of this chapter, so that if unbelievers were to enter a Christian gathering, they would not think everyone was crazy (14:23) or that everybody was indecent or lived in disorder (14:40). The command that women remain silent is not a goal in itself. It exists so that the church in Corinth would not become a stumbling block for Jews or Gentiles.

Final Considerations

Just as in the cases of slavery and rape that we mentioned earlier, the question about female leadership in the church is not part of an idle debate that wants to continue making problematic a situation that has always been difficult. It is simply that, while we follow the Lord and see him act, we do not see that it is possible to maintain gender inequalities in his presence. The disciplines that "explain the present" show that these debates emerged from the most deeply painful times in history.

---

20. Aristophanes, Lys. 505–520, in: Aristophanes, *Lysistrata, The Women's Festival, and Frogs*, Trans. Michael Ewans, (University of Oklahoma Press, 2010), 73–74.

Do our hearts tremble when we analyze our customs regarding the leadership of women? Are we uncomfortable and troubled in spirit when we tell a woman that, in spite of all her abilities, in obedience to a biblical command, she cannot fulfill a task of church leadership, for example? Apparently, what the debate about female leadership raises again and again is precisely this intuition of the church that something does not "fit" with the way we interpret the text and spirit of Christ.

This is not the first time that the church has gone beyond the plain reading of the Bible when it is following the Spirit's leading. Neither is it the first time that the church has made a mistake by practicing the plain reading of Scripture. According to Ronald Pierce, it was a plain reading of Psalm 104:5 and Isaiah 51:16 which led Luther, Calvin, Owen, and Wesley to condemn Galileo's ideas. In a similar way, it was a plain reading of Genesis 3:16 which led many to consider a woman to be a heretic if she received any kind of medical assistance during childbirth.[21]

The study of the Bible era shows, with great clarity, that the gender roles one perceives in the Bible are not a Christian invention, but rather a reflection of the era. There is no other way for this to happen. As we stated above, if the word of God had not been communicated in the language and culture shared by its first readers, it would have been incomprehensible and impractical. The task for the student of the Bible is to seek the eternal message that comes to us hidden in vessels of clay, but not to confuse the precious message with the vessel.[22]

---

21. Ronald W. Pierce, "Evangelicals and Gender Roles in the 1990s: 1 Tim 2:8–15 – A Test Case," *Journal of the Evangelical Theological Society* 36, no. 3 (1993): 345.

22. The following studies address the topic in anthropological, social, and cultural ways: Rafael Aguirre, "La casa como estructura base del cristianismo primitivo: las iglesias domesticas," *Estudios Eclesiásticos* 59, no. 228 (1984): 27–51; Rafael Aguirre, *Del movimiento de Jesús a la iglesia cristiana: Ensayo de exëgesis sociológica del cristianismo primitivo* (Estella: Verbo Divino, 1998); Richard A. Horsley, "Popular Prophetic Movements at the Time of Jesus: Their Principal Features and Social Origins," *Journal for the Study of the New Testament* 8, no. 26 (1986): 3–27; Richard A. Horsley, *Jesús y el Imperio: El reino de Dios y el nuevo desorden mundial*, Agora 14 (Estella: Verbo Divino, 2003); Richard A. Horsley, "Religion and Other Products of Empire," *Journal of the American Academy of Religion* 71, no. 1 (2003): 13–44; Malina, *El mundo del Nuevo Testamento*; Malina, *El mundo social de Jesús y los evangelios*; Luther H. Martin, *Hellenistic Religions: An Introduction* (New York: Oxford University Press, 1987); Emil Schürer, *Historia del Pueblo Judío en Tiempos de Jesús, 175 a.C. – 135 d.C.: Fuentes y marco histórico*, vol. 1 (Madrid: Cristiandad, 1985); Emil Schürer, *Historia del Pueblo Judío en Tiempos de Jesús: Instituciones políticas y religiosas*, vol. 2 (Madrid: Cristiandad, 1985); Dennis Edwin Smith, *Del simposio a la eucaristía: El banquete en el mundo cristiano antiguo*, Agora 26 (Estella: Verbo Divino, 2009); Stegemann and Stegemann, *Historia social del cristianismo*; Gerd Theissen, *La religión de los primeros cristianos: Una teoría del cristianismo primitivo* (Salamanca: Sígueme, 2002).

References

Aguirre, Rafael. "La casa como estructura base del cristianismo primitivo: las iglesias domesticas." *Estudios Eclesiásticos* 59, no. 228 (1984): 27–51.

———. *Del movimiento de Jesús a la iglesia cristiana: Ensayo de exëgesis sociológica del cristianismo primitivo.* Estella: Verbo Divino, 1998.

Aristophanes, *Lysistrata, The Women's Festival, and Frogs*, Trans. Michael Ewans, University of Oklahoma Press, 2010.

Culver, Robert D. "Una postura tradicionalista: 'Las mujeres guarden silencio.'" In *Mujeres en el Ministerio*, edited by Bonnidell Clouse and Robert G. Clouse, 31–57. Barcelona: CLIE, 2005.

Foh, Susan T. "Una postura en pro del liderazgo masculino, 'La cabeza de la mujer es el hombre.'" In *Mujeres en el ministerio*, edited by Bonnidell Clouse and Robert G. Clouse, 69–119. Barcelona: CLIE, 2005.

Hensley, Adam. "Σιγαω, Λαλεω, and ὑποτασσω in 1 Corinthians 14:34 in Their Literary and Rhetorical Context." *Journal of the Evangelical Theological Society* 55, no. 2 (2012): 343–64.

Horsley, Richard A. *Jesús y el Imperio: El reino de Dios y el nuevo desorden mundial.* Agora 14. Estella: Verbo Divino, 2003.

———. "Popular Prophetic Movements at the Time of Jesus: Their Principal Features and Social Origins." *Journal for the Study of the New Testament* 8, no. 26 (1986): 3–27.

———. "Religion and Other Products of Empire." *Journal of the American Academy of Religion* 71, no. 1 (2003): 13–44.

MacArthur, John. "Can Women Exercise Authority in the Church?" Grace to You. 29 August 2013. https://www.gty.org/library/blog/B130829/can-women-exercise-authority-in-the-church.

Malina, Bruce J. *El mundo del Nuevo Testamento: Perspectivas desde la antropología cultural.* Agora 1. Estella: Verbo Divino, 1995.

———. *El mundo social de Jesús y los evangelios: La antropología cultural mediterránea y el Nuevo Testamento.* Presencia Teológica 116. Santander: Sal Terrae, 2002.

Martin, Luther H. *Hellenistic Religions: An Introduction.* New York: Oxford University Press, 1987.

Murphy-O'Connor, J. "1 Corinthians 11:2–16 Once Again." *The Catholic Biblical Quarterly* 50, no. 2 (1988): 265–74.

Padgett, Alan. "Paul on Women in the Church: The Contradictions of Coiffure in 1 Corinthians 11:2–16." *Journal for the Study of the New Testament* 6, no. 20 (1984): 69–86.

Pierce, Ronald W. "Evangelicals and Gender Roles in the 1990s: 1 Tim 2:8–15 – A Test Case." *Journal of the Evangelical Theological Society* 36, no. 3 (1993): 343–55.

Schürer, Emil. *Historia del Pueblo Judío en Tiempos de Jesús, 175 a.C. – 135 d.C.: Fuentes y marco histórico.* Vol. 1. Madrid: Cristiandad, 1985.

———. *Historia del Pueblo Judío en Tiempos de Jesús: Instituciones políticas y religiosas.* Vol. 2. Madrid: Cristiandad, 1985.

Segundo, Juan Luis. *Liberación de la Teología.* Cuadernos Latinoamericanos. Buenos Aires: Carlo Lohle, 1975.

Smith, Dennis Edwin. *Del simposio a la eucaristía: El banquete en el mundo cristiano antiguo.* Agora 26. Estella: Verbo Divino, 2009.

Stegemann, E. W., and W. Stegemann. *Historia social del cristianismo primitivo: Los inicios en el judaísmo y las comunidades cristianas.* Agora 8. Estella: Verbo Divino, 2008.

Theissen, Gerd. *La religión de los primeros cristianos: Una teoría del cristianismo primitivo.* Salamanca: Sígueme, 2002.

5

Reading the Bible "Naturally"

Loving God and Your Neighbor through a Contextual Hermeneutic (Matthew 19:1–12)

Juan José Barreda Toscano

> "To fly a kite[1] in this storm
> only leads to the conclusion that yesterday is not today
> and today is today,
> and that I am not the actor that I used to be."
> "Spaguetti del Rock," Divididos

3. Final Syntheses[2]

10. Matthew 19:1–12 is not a teaching text about divorce. It is the narrative of a scene of public dispute about divorce. Jesus is responding to a very specific question.

9. It is a mistake to treat the topic of marital abandonment outside of the marriage context of the era.

8. The concept of family in the first century AD was very different from the idea of family in Western cultures today. Many of the healthy practices that are

---

1. "Remontar un barrilete" is used by the band Divididos to refer to the act of flying a kite. It is principally used in Argentina.

2. "Do not be afraid", the reverse order of numbering in this chapter is intentional.

recommended for engagement or marriage today would have been considered immoral in the first century.

7. All interpretations of the Bible are contextual. It is impossible to literally fulfill biblical perspectives about marriage and marital repudiation/abandonment given the social, economic, cultural, and religious changes that have occurred. To say that being "biblical" means practicing even the smallest details of the customs around the family in biblical times is a fallacy.

6. In public discussions, Jesus was influenced by the active and dynamic presence of women. A solid interpretation of the text should not ignore this fact.

5. Jesus appealed to the fundamental texts of Genesis 1 and 2 to point out the theological foundations of equality and mutual care in marriage, not to inaugurate (affirm) an indissoluble institution.

4. Matthew 19:1–12 deals with divorce or "repudiation," a concept of the marriage bond that only the man was legally able to put into effect. The woman did not have the legal right to do this.

3. Jesus rejected divorce for just "any reason," but not for certain reasons in specific situations.

2. The "exception clause" of verse 9 demonstrates by its very existence that Jesus did not consider marriage to be (totally) indissoluble.

1. Contextual hermeneutics permit us to be more just with regards to the real-life experiences of marriage. Literalist methods of interpretation, even more so when they are accompanied by legalist perspectives, present a "Jesus" far removed from the Christ presented in the four Gospels.

2. A Contextual Analysis of Matthew 19:1–12

A contextual analysis of Matthew 19:1–12 has not been developed much in Latin American biblical studies,[3] at least not in a way that would take into consideration recent contributions from other fields of study. Writings in Latin American pastoral psychology, with few exceptions, do not even mention the topic of divorce. We recognize that divorce is a delicate topic. The evangelical

---

3. One recent example is the book by Eduardo Arens, ¿Hasta que la muerte los separe? El divorcio en el Nuevo Testamento (Navarra: Verbo Divino, 2015).

church has tended to deny the reality of divorce, or to present it as an "attack" against the institution of the family. For example, the Gospel Coalition has recently promoted its view of marriage, and as a consequence, of divorce. They utilize a "literalist" method of biblical interpretation with a legalistic tone.[4] This perspective does not do justice either to the reality of the circumstances of divorces, nor to the allusions and teaching about divorce that we have in the Scriptures.

In what follows, we will explore a contextual hermeneutic of Matthew 19:1–10. We will utilize some recent contextual hermeneutical tools and methods. We will also approach the text from an empathetic approach, striving to "hear the voices" of those who usually are silent. We do this in an attempt to love them as a way of following the testimony of Jesus.

Notes Regarding Families in Judea and Galilee in the First Century AD

We would make a mistake if we read this passage without first trying to understand the families and marriages that we are studying. This should be apparent because the breakup of a marriage presupposes the prior existence of that marriage.[5] Galilean and Jewish families of that period were quite different from the urban, Westernized ones of our day. Even the way people usually got married would be antithetical to the way evangelical, Westernized families are formed today, even the most conservative ones. Many of the practices that are recommended today as healthy and "biblical" – understood in a literal sense – would have been seen in the first century as "indecent" and "sinful" (to meet and get to know your future spouse prior to the wedding, for the wife to work in employment outside the home, etc.).

In many cases, marriages were arranged by the parents, sometimes in response to an initiative taken by the children, but frequently without consulting

---

4. For example, see John Piper in Riquezas de Gracia, "¿Dios permite doble nupcias si hubo adulterio?," https://www.youtube.com/watch?v=CUsWrn0PNtg; or Miguel Núñez in Solo por Gracia, "Miguel Núñez: El divorcio según la Biblia," YouTube, accessed 17 September 2020, https://www.youtube.com/watch?v=vtoHKlYqlxw. By "legalism," I refer to the practice of excluding the subjective character of any interpretation, in which the literary genre of a text is ignored and the interpretation is cast as a "law or norm." To achieve this, an appeal is made to the artifice of a "literal" interpretation, which is a fallacy presented as being faithful to the sacred text but ignores the very nature of that text by imposing upon it an ideological essence and message.

5. Regarding this background, see the work of Shaye J. D. Cohen, ed., *The Jewish Family in Antiquity* (Atlanta: Scholars, 1993); Tal Ilan, *Jewish Women in Greco-Roman Palestine* (Peabody: Hendrickson, 1996); Halvor Moxnes, ed., *Constructing Early Christian Families: Family as Social Reality and Metaphor* (London: Routledge, 1997).

them at all. It is thought that a young woman would be given in marriage when she was about fourteen, and the young man would be about eighteen. The woman would transition from being under the authority of her father to being under that of her husband. Marriage was understood as the acquisition of the woman; the husband was her lord. The goals of a marriage were to have children, to increase and protect the family property, and, if possible, to love each other. In extended families, which were not uncommon in those days, the young couple would live under the leadership of the paternal family's patriarch. The young wife, in particular, should adapt to the leadership of the older women in her husband's family. Personal freedoms within marriages were unthinkable in those times. Therefore, the word "submit" was used to describe marital relations.

Concubinage and polygamy were common expressions in marriage in those times. It was unlikely that those who came to Jesus would have referred only to monogamous families. What would a rupture look like in the dissolution of a relationship with a concubine? Generally, those who analyze Matthew 19:1–12 fail to raise the question whether the answers given by Jesus included concubines or not. Another serious reference deals with the situation of sons and daughters. Differences between a son and a daughter were enormous.[6] On the other hand, male and female slaves were also part of the "household."[7] Female slaves, from a very young age, were kept for the sexual use of their masters as part of their "domestic" duties. What would the marital relationship among slaves look like? Would Jesus have been thinking only about free people, given that the percentage of the population who were slaves was very high in the first century AD?[8] Definitely not. When a passage like Matthew 19 is studied, it is important to think about this diverse audience in public discussion. To not take this diverse public into consideration can easily lead to a distortion of Jesus and his teachings.

What Is Matthew 19:1–12?

Matthew 19:1–12 is not a "doctrine manual" nor a "penalty code" regarding the prohibition against divorce. It is very important to correctly identify the literary genre of a biblical passage if you want to interpret it appropriately and use it

---

6. Sirach 22:3 says, "It is a disgrace to be the father of an undisciplined son, and the birth of a daughter is a loss" (NRSV). For additional insights see Ilan, *Jewish Women*, 44–56.

7. Jennifer A. Glancy, *Slavery in Early Christianity* (Minneapolis: Fortress, 2006), 9–38.

8. Dale B. Martin, "Slavery and Ancient Jewish Family," in Cohen, *Jewish Family*, 118.

for blessing and not to do further damage. Our passage in Matthew explicitly tells us that it narrates a public dispute and it uses an appropriate form and structure (cf. Matt 4:1–11; 22:15–22, 23–33). The structure follows a pattern that is similar to that of other texts of public argument.[9] That pattern "typified the relations between men in societies based on the binomial of honor/shame."[10] This passage is a discussion initiated by the Pharisees in an attempt to discredit Jesus as a teacher.

It is not a moment when Jesus wanted to teach about divorce within a marriage. The text explicitly states that it is a dispute, and it is presented as a tense situation. It has proposals that are aimed at trapping Jesus, and he gives brief, short answers. This is far from a thoughtful teaching setting that would lend itself to thoughtful reflection. Although it is true that it expresses some of Jesus's views on divorce, it would be wrong to think that we will find in this passage Jesus's total teaching regarding marriage and divorce. To do so would be to distort the passage, thus forcing it to "teach" something that it did not really teach.

A comparative analysis of Matthew 19:1–12 and Mark 10:1–12 provides us with a very important piece of information. The majority of Bible specialists follow the "hypothesis of the sources" which states that Matthew 19 used Mark 10 as its basis.[11] Over the last decades, other theories have gained prominence. These explain that the many similarities between the two passages are probably due to both gospel writers utilizing common oral traditions that existed prior to the written composition of either writing.[12] For the analysis of our text, both theories are helpful to explain the points in common and the differences between the two passages. A common mistake is made when interpretations are made from an interspersed reading, without taking into consideration the sections that are unique to each version. We will comment on this later in the chapter.

---

9. This is pointed out by David Instone-Brewer, *Divorce and Remarriage in the Bible: The Social and Literary Context* (Grand Rapids: Eerdmans, 2002), 173.

10. Bruce J. Malina and Richard L. Rohrbaugh, *Los evangelios sinópticos y la cultura mediterránea del siglo 1* (Navarra: Verbo Divino, 2002), 96.

11. A. Vargas Machuca, "La llamada Fuente Q de los Evangelios Sinópticos," in *Fuentes del cristianismo: Tradiciones primitivas del sobre Jesús*, ed. Antonio Piñero (Córdoba: El Almendro, 1993), 63–94.

12. James D. G. Dunn, *Jesus Remembered*, vol. 1 of *Christianity in the Making* (Grand Rapids: Eerdmans, 2003), 210–54.

Analysis of Matthew 19:1–12

Matthew uses a rhetorical device in which Jesus is depicted as a foreigner who leaves his home ("he left Galilee," v. 1) and is now interacting with the people of Judea as he makes his way to Jerusalem. He is greatly accepted by the general population ("large crowds," v. 2), but there is also opposition from the Pharisees. In contrast to Mark, Matthew includes a private conversation that Jesus has with the Galilean disciples who express nonconformity with some of Jesus's teaching (vv. 10–12). Two facts are important: the multitudes were following Jesus, and he healed them (v. 2). While Mark states that Jesus was teaching (10:1), Matthew highlights his ministry of healing-salvation of the multitudes, an action which denotes the messianic nature of his ministry. Jesus is a religious authority for the people, one who can guide them. It is within this context that we perceive that the Pharisees' actions are neither neutral nor accidental. The passage describes them as a group who want to test Jesus in order to discredit him. They possibly think that as Jesus's popularity grows, their own influence will decline. They test Jesus by asking him a question that will pit him against the men, by disrupting the privileged place of men in an institution where patriarchal power was quite evident: marriage.

"Is it lawful for a man to divorce his wife *for any and every reason*?" (v. 3b, emphasis added). The question in Matthew differs from that of Mark in the circumstances, adding "for any and every reason." The question in Mark asks about the viability (or not) of divorce, whereas in Matthew it is about causes that would justify divorce. Nevertheless, some specialists consider that Mark is essentially asking the same question as in Matthew. Matthew adds this clarification for those of his readers who might not be aware of Jewish culture and might not understand the core issue in the question as it appears in Mark 10:2.[13] Nevertheless, there are various differences between the texts that demonstrate that there was more at stake than merely clarifying what the original question was. It shows there were different positions that developed regarding divorce.

Here I will highlight some important points in Matthew 19:1–12 that are frequently omitted in literal interpretations. First, the question assumes that divorce was an accepted practice in all known Jewish groups. In the second

---

13. For example, Instone-Brewer, *Divorce and Remarriage*, 175. On the other hand, Arens and others follow the view that Matthew and Mark describe different questions. See Arens, *¿Hasta que la muerte los separe?*, 106–7. If this view is accurate, we are witnesses to various understandings of divorce in the New Testament together with what Paul shares in 1 Corinthians 7. This reflects the complexity of the issue, and how the early church shared various points of view regarding this life situation.

place, the woman could not divorce her husband regardless of who he was or what he had done (with few exceptions). Third, what she could do was to ask the town elders to request the husband to divorce her, but the final decision was always in the hands of the husband. Fourth, when all was said and done, for a woman to divorce her husband seems to have occurred only in the most exceptional cases,[14] or if she belonged to the wealthy elite with special privileges. Most women in that society did not have the possibility of divorcing their husbands. This was the unjust, asymmetrical relationship that existed between a husband and wife.

In the fifth place the translation of the Greek verb *apolusai* (divorce, expel, repudiate) is important. The contextual semantic importance of *apolusai* refers to the right that only the man had and the social stigma that fell upon the ex-wife as a woman who was thrown out of the house. The woman ended up in a position of social shame, with society's criticism of her fitness as a woman and wife.[15] It is not known for certain if the woman could keep her children. It is likely that they stayed with the father, unless they were expelled together with the mother. If the woman did not have a relative who would receive her into his or her home, she would quickly need to find another husband, or offer herself as a servant or concubine to a man who could provide her with food and lodging (see John 4:17–18: "You are right . . . the man you now have is not your husband"). The verb *apolusai* does not allude merely to "divorcing," but means to "repudiate" or "expel" the wife. To use the verb "divorce" in English (or Spanish) tends to distort what really happened historically. This also tends to distort what Jesus was actually rejecting in this specific context.

A sixth point consists in discerning why the Pharisees used this topic in their attempt to discredit Jesus. It is frequently claimed that behind this question are the differences regarding divorce between two schools of thought, the House of Shammai and the House of Hillel.[16] We don't know for sure to

---

14. See the articles published regarding the topic in Bernard S. Jackson, ed., *The Jewish Law Annual*, Vol. 4 (Leiden: Brill, 1981).

15. Rabbi Meir, in a text dated around AD 150, stated: "Whoever marries a woman divorced by her husband for her shameful conduct is worthy of death, because he has accepted a ruined woman into his home" (b. Giṭ. 90b). Feminine sexuality was suspect, as can be seen in the literature of the period. See Juan José Barreda Toscano, "Textos en la literatura Intertestamentaria sobre la sexualidad en la pareja," *Palabra y Vida* 3 (2019): 11–26, https://www.unireformada.edu.co/wp-content/uploads/2017/12/CUR.RevistaPalabrayVida.No3-2019-.pdf.

16. m. Giṭ 9:10: "The House of Shammai say, 'A man should divorce his wife only because he has found grounds for it in unchastity,' since it is said, 'Because he has found in her indecency in anything (Dt. 24:).' And the House of Hillel say, 'Even if she spoiled his dish,' since it is said, 'Because he has found in her indecency in anything.' R. Aqiba says, 'Even if he found someone else prettier than she,' since it is said, 'And it shall be if she find no favor in his eyes

what extent these two interpretations regarding divorce had filtered down to the common people. Nevertheless, we need to recognize that the two interpretations were based upon the same ideological foundation: patriarchy. The Pharisees' question was raised to place Jesus in opposition to the interests of the majority of men. They wanted to pit Jesus against men. The trap in this question is that his answer could divide the multitude by contrasting the interests of men with those of women. The reaction of his disciples in 19:10 reinforces this idea: "If this is the situation between a husband and wife, it is better not to marry." This verse does not reflect a doctrinal teaching. This is a tense dispute with Jesus's strategic answers. The topic of divorce is a pretext to address a deeper problem: the power of men over women in marriage – and in society. The Pharisees expected that this dispute would end with Jesus setting himself against the people's fundamental practices which were "God's will." They partially achieved their goal.

And What Did the Women Think?

Feminist hermeneutics have helped interpret biblical texts from the perspectives and active presence of women in the Jesus movement.[17] Frequently, the biblical texts do not mention these women, or they refer to them anonymously.[18] It is an ethically healthy hermeneutical task to visualize and imagine their presence, their interests, and their possible opinions.[19] It is interesting to note, as an example, that Pastor Miguel Núñez makes an effort to contextualize these passages to a certain extent. He states that a woman who has suffered the adultery of her husband "can" divorce him even though the text does not literally affirm this. Nevertheless, this timid contextualization results in a legalistic perspective that does not permit going deeper in the analysis of the topic. It falls into a legalism that wants to see the phrase "except for sexual immorality" as an extreme and the only justification.[20]

(Dt. 24:1)." Jacob Neusner, *The Mishnah: A New Translation* (New Haven, CT: Yale University Press, 1988), 487.

17. See the work of Elaine M. Wainwright, *Shall We Look for Another? A Feminist Rereading of the Matthean Jesus* (New York: Orbis, 1988).

18. Silvia Pellegrini, "Mujeres sin nombre en los evangelios canónicos," in *Los Evangelios: Narraciones e historia*, ed. M. Navarro y M. Perroni (Navarra: Verbo Divino, 2011), 393–432.

19. Elizabeth Schüssler-Fiorenza, "The Ethics of Biblical Interpretation: Decentering Biblical Scholarship," *Journal of Biblical Literature* 107 (1988): 3–17.

20. Again, I recommend viewing the YouTube video of Núñez cited in note 4 above. John Piper's perspectives (also see note 4) are even more extreme.

As we return to our text, it is essential to acknowledge that "the large crowds" would have included wives, mothers, grandmothers, concubines, and female slaves and servants who lived the reality of marriage and, of course, had their own opinions about marriage. The Pharisees' question within this scenario is, itself, an aggression. These women are presented as objects of possession whose opinions and interests are not worthy to be considered. Theologically speaking, the question implies that God shows favoritism toward men. Socially, it treats women as possessions, to the point that it ignores their opinions and assumes that men have the right to make decisions for them.

It is important to ask a question about the expression "Is it lawful?"[21] Who determines what is lawful? Which beliefs is it based upon? The Pharisees appeal to traditions they consider normative that do not include women in the decision-making but have perspectives on and make decisions about them.[22] The perspectives they share about masculinity and the role of men reveal there was no consensus. There is another point that is frequently not acknowledged. To ignore the dynamic and active presence of women in this scenario is a hermeneutical option, not an obvious fact. We do not know for sure why neither Matthew nor Mark mentioned women, but it is true that their verbal and nonverbal participation in these events existed but was not included.[23] It is more in agreement with the ministry of Jesus to think that the presence of women shaped his decision regarding what was really happening.[24] When we approach more specifically the women in this multitude, the topic of divorce becomes quite complicated and requires greater sensitivity and contextualization to adequately interpret Matthew 19:1–12.

Various exegetes state that Jesus's answer favored the wives. But it is possible that he did so not in the way that they expected. Why would a woman feel favored if she knew that her husband was obligated to stay with her, even if he did not love her any longer and did not want to keep her at his side (cf. 1 Cor 7:15)? And what about those women who were abused

---

21. Werner Foerster reminds us: "In the New Testament, ἔξεστιν relates most commonly to the Law and will of God." Werner Foerster, "ἔξεστιν," in *Theological Dictionary of the New Testament*, vol. 2, eds. Gerhard Kittel and Gerhard Friedrich, translated by Geoffrey W. Bromiley (Grand Rapids: Eerdmans, 1964–1976), 561.

22. Tal Ilan points out: "Pharisaism, particularly the kind reflected in rabbinic literature, seems extremely hostile toward women and women's status in society," *Integrating Women into Second Temple History* (Peabody: Hendrickson, 2001), 31–32.

23. Anthony J. Saldarini, "Mujeres ausentes en los hogares de Mateo," in *Una compañera para Mateo*, ed. A. J. Levine (Bilbao: Desclée de Brouwer, 2003), 247–65.

24. Ivone Richter Raimer, "'No temaís . . . id a ver . . . y anunciad': Mujeres en el Evangelio de Mateo," *Revista de Interpretación Bíblica Latinoamericana* 27 (1997): 145–61.

physically, psychologically, or socioeconomically (cf. Exod 21:10–11)? Would they consider Jesus's answer as something that benefited them? Perhaps some of them felt for a moment that Jesus had betrayed them.

And Jesus's proposal: Did it really require the husband to stay with his wife in order to "save the marriage" at all costs? Was Jesus a defender of the social establishment? The legalistic and literalistic interpretation of Matthew 19:1–12 invents a "Jesus" who is quite different from the one we know in the rest of Matthew's gospel. That "Jesus" demands a fulfillment of the law without considering how it would impact the lives of people. That kind of "Jesus" would dishearten the people because he would not be considering their actual lives. For example, John Piper, interpreting Matthew 19 in relation to Ephesians 5, maintains that a woman whose adulterous husband returns to her and is sincerely repentant should not leave him because the Lord never divorces his bride – the church – even after her adulteries.[25] Legalism distorts the biblical text and pushes it to present an image of Jesus that is not realistic. How does this legalistic Jesus square with our Savior who broke with social and family norms? Wouldn't this undermine the freedoms inspired by his gospel? Is this legalistic "Jesus" the same who asked: Who is my mother, and who are my brothers and sisters? And extending his hand toward his disciples, said: Behold, here are my brothers and sisters, because everyone who does the will of my Father that is in heaven is my brother, and sister, and mother (see Matt 12:48–50; cf. 10:34–36)?[26] The Jesus whom Matthew's gospel presents to us and who invites us to build healthy family relationships or who criticized situations of injustice (cf. Matt 5–7) is impossible to reconcile with the authoritarian and insensitive "Jesus" of the literalistic interpretation.

Therefore, What Did Jesus Say?

Matthew 19:4–8 differs from Mark 10:3–9 in the order of the answers that Jesus gave. The first remark that Jesus provided in Matthew did not respond to the Pharisees' question. He ethically disagreed with the question, and therefore criticized it. Then he addressed the heart of the problem: the patriarchy expressed in the asymmetrical relationship in marriage.

---

25. See the Piper YouTube video in note 4. Let's be clear. The issue here is not whether the woman should stay with her adulterous husband. Piper's mistake is that he ignores the specific case, the right of the woman to decide based upon her freedom in Christ and the terrible damage that she has experienced in her marriage.

26. Halvor Moxnes, *Poner a Jesús en su lugar: Una visión radical del grupo familiar y el Reino de Dios* (Navarra: Verbo Divino, 2005).

"Haven't you read . . . that at the beginning the Creator 'made them male and female' . . . ?" He begins by quoting Genesis 1, making use of a hermeneutical resource practiced within Judaism at that time: the older text has more authority than the more recent one. Genesis 1 is older than Deuteronomy 24. God is greater than Moses. With this text, Jesus points out the equality of woman and man. Both have been created in the image and likeness of God. His argument is fundamentally theological. It is not biological, nor sociological, nor psychological.[27] He appeals to a sacred, normative text: God made them as equals.[28]

The syntactic phrase "and [he] said" (v. 5) shows the connection between, and not the mixing of, the earlier quote and the one that follows. Given the hermeneutical criterion that the oldest text has priority, the second quote is subordinated to the first: "For this reason a man will leave his father and mother and be united to his wife, and the two will become one flesh." "For this reason" (Grk *heneka*) subjects what follows to what came before. Because they are a pair, the union of the woman and the man constitutes a relationship based upon equality and mutual well-being (cf. Gen 1:28). Jesus appeals to the marriage covenant as a union as strong as blood ("one flesh"). This is an ethical and voluntary relationship. Jesus breaks with a "biologistic" or deterministic understanding of family relations. Marriage is the exercise of God's ideal of the relationship between those who have become one. It is not a fossilized institution. To divorce one's wife would mean, in this social context, "to repudiate her." This would be to expose her to shame and to leave her without the resources she needs for living. This would put her in a degrading situation given the structures that were hostile to women in that society. Jesus did not seem to have a problem with the dissolution of marriage, but he did have a problem with the repudiation aspect of divorce.

"Why then . . . did Moses command [Grk *eneteilato*] that a man give his wife a certificate of divorce and send her away?" The Pharisees, resorting to their interpretation of the text of Deuteronomy 24:1–4, create a command: repudiate your wife if something is found in her that is indecent. Their discussion becomes a hermeneutical issue. Jesus clarifies that Moses "permitted"

---

27. See the psychological and sociological arguments used by Ben Sira to maintain the inferiority of women to men. Maurice Gilbert, *Ben Sira: Recueil d'études* (Leuven: Peeters, 2014), 249–64.

28. There is clear evidence that already in the first century AD there was a distinction within Judaism between a normative sacred writing and the interpretations of this text by the elders. Juan José Barreda Toscano, *La Comunidad de Qumrán y los dos Mesías* (Buenos Aires: La Aurora, 2019), 98–100, 341–43.

(Grk *epetrepsen*) men to divorce their wives but did not command this. And then Jesus directly accuses the Pharisees: "because *your* hearts were hard," and "you . . . divorce *your* wives." Jesus does not follow the hermeneutical fallacy of objectivity. He connects the interpretation of the sacred text with the subjectivity of the interpreters. He does not question subjectivity in itself, but he does criticize it because it comes from people with "hard hearts." Within this context he says, "Anyone who divorces his wife . . . and marries another woman commits adultery."

Much has been written about the so-called "exception clause" and about the meaning of "sexual immorality" or "fornication" (Grk *porneia*, v. 9). Studies show that this word had a variety of meanings. In general, it referred to an unacceptable sexual practice according to the ethics in a specific cultural and religious context. Its possible meanings are so diverse that it can include adultery.[29] We do not know for sure its exact meaning in 19:9. We should understand that it clearly refers to a sexual offense against the husband. The question should be asked whether looking for one specific meaning of *porneia* is helpful and whether Jesus referred literally only to the translation of *porneia* as "fornication." Wouldn't this ignore the complexity of human relationships? On the other hand, we should ask why Jesus would consider a sexual issue as the only valid cause for divorce within a marriage. What is most important in this passage is the very existence of the exception clause. This indicates that, for Jesus, marriage could be ended. Therefore, other causes could ethically be justification for divorce (such as physical violence, sexual abuse, psychological mistreatment, delinquency, affective indifference . . .).

A contextual interpretation of Matthew 19:9 helps us to better understand Jesus in light of the image described by Matthew in the rest of his gospel. It shows us that this passage does not cover all that Jesus thought about marriage, nor the justifiable causes for its dissolution. Jesus does not demonstrate that he is in favor of or against divorce in itself, just as he is neither in favor of nor against marriage. On the other hand, the existence of this exception clause shows us that his perspective was not to deepen the suffering of women already in situations of great suffering. "What God has joined together, let no one separate" (v. 6) highlights the divine ideal, not a sacramental or legal formula. He refers to a path to follow, a healthy union, and, therefore, an exhortation for how to maintain the marriage relationship that claims to be united by God.

---

29. See the diverse list of interpretations of *porneia* in Evald Lövestam, "Divorce and Remarriage in the New Testament," *The Jewish Law Annual*, vol. 4, ed. Bernard S. Jackson (Leiden: Brill, 1981), 53–58.

The final scene of Matthew 19:10–12 continues in this direction. As was mentioned earlier, the disciples reveal their nonconformity, but Jesus goes to the heart of the matter. He addresses the topic of the social impositions about the family that go against an abundant life. The theme of these verses is not about "chastity." It is rather about the freedom to build family relationships outside of the bonds of marriage. This is what Jesus himself did by becoming family with other followers whom he loved and who loved him (cf. Matt 12:48–50). Jesus proposes that they reject the paradigm of masculinity that was based on dominion over women and which reduced women to being sexual objects. Jesus proposes that they assume the abundant life by relating to women in friendship and fellowship as equals as a witness to and proclamation of the kingdom of God.

1. Reading the Bible "Naturally"

Every reading of the Bible is an exercise in interpretation, both subjective and contextual. As human beings situated in the world, it is not possible to read the Scriptures without doing so contextually. It is not an option; it is an inevitable fact. In reality, what we can do is choose how we read the Bible contextually. We should do so fully aware of the limitations and human possibilities that come with the process of knowing God through the Scriptures. Therefore, reading the Bible naturally should be an exercise in humility before God and our neighbors. It is a dialogue, with oneself, in community, and with/from the biblical text. As such, it is also an ethical exercise, a way to love our neighbor if we decide to follow the spirit of Jesus.[30]

Thanks to the subjectivity and contextual nature of the reading of the Bible, we can communicate, or at least connect, with the biblical text. This means we can identify with the biblical stories, and we can grab hold of them, and let them grab hold of us![31] Without subjectivity, there would be no way we could say, "This is what God is saying to us," and without a contextual reading, it would be impossible to rethink our biblical reflections in order to live them out in our world. Guided by God's Spirit, we need to return to a natural reading of the Bible, with our feet firmly planted on the ground, and

---

30. For a long time, Latin American biblical hermeneutics have been seen as examples of justice and love for one's neighbor. I recommend the work of Hans de Wit, *Por un solo gesto de amor: Lectura de la Biblia desde una práctica intercultural* (Buenos Aires: IU ISEDET 2006), especially chapter 7, "El otro como lugar epifánico," 259–304.

31. See the concept of the hermeneutics of appropriation in Severino Croatto, *Hermenéutica práctica* (Buenos Aires: Lumen, 2002).

allowing God to be God. An analysis of texts like Matthew 19:1–12 teaches us how enriching and challenging it can be to study the Bible contextually. This means getting to know God through dialogue, through a dance of stories and biblical testimonies with which we can create new patterns. When we read the Scriptures under the guidance of the *parakletos* we are led by the Spirit in an exercise of community remembrance of Jesus (cf. John 14–16).[32] This is a remembrance that involves those who were eyewitnesses with the original disciples, and which permits us to join with them in following the spirit of Jesus who came to give life and life in abundance.

Reading the Bible naturally is the sublime call to plant our feet on the ground, to be aware of our finitude, and to know God from a position of humility. If there is a warning to heed from the interpretation of Matthew 19:1–12, it is that we can cause great damage if we respond from an attitude of authoritarianism and exclusion, whether it is in the interpreter or in Jesus himself. But we also see that a contextual interpretation connects us with the Jesus who loved, who invited us to follow him in this task. Many divorced people hope for a Jesus who, at least, sincerely listens to them, who shows true greatness by listening carefully to them, who understands them, and who would shepherd them. But a legalist Jesus is presented to them, one who pressures them to fulfill a precept that did not contemplate their reasons or their situations. This Jesus makes them suffer even more. This Jesus pushes them away from the churches.

In our current context of marriage in our societies, what would Jesus teach about divorce? What response would Pharisees suggest today? And what vision of marriage would Jesus propose? I hope that we have solid answers for these questions. The current context challenges us to bring the Jesus of Matthew 19:1–12 into the lives of so many abandoned people. It challenges us to love our neighbors through a contextual hermeneutic that encourages an opening of doors so that people can enter – so that they may talk with open hearts and can feel his hug telling them that he came to accompany them.

References

Arens, Eduardo. *¿Hasta que la muerte los separe? El divorcio en el Nuevo Testamento.* Navarra: Verbo Divino, 2015.

---

32. I recommend reading this excellent study: Javier Ortega, *El Evangelio de Juan y la Iglesia (im)posible: Política eclesial a la luz de Juan 13–17* (Madrid: San Pablo, 2019), 198–200.

Barreda Toscano, Juan José. *La Comunidad de Qumrán y los dos Mesías.* Buenos Aires: La Aurora, 2019.

———. "Textos en la literatura Intertestamentaria sobre la sexualidad en la pareja." *Palabra y Vida* 3 (2019): 11–26. https://www.unireformada.edu.co/wp-content/uploads/2017/12/CUR.RevistaPalabrayVida.No3-2019-.pdf.

Cohen, Shaye J. D., ed. *The Jewish Family in Antiquity.* Atlanta: Scholars, 1993.

Croatto, Severino. *Hermenéutica práctica.* Buenos Aires: Lumen, 2002.

de Wit, Hans. *Por un solo gesto de amor: Lectura de la Biblia desde una práctica intercultural.* Buenos Aires: IU ISEDET, 2006.

Dunn, James D. G. *Jesus Remembered.* Vol. 1 of *Christianity in the Making.* Grand Rapids: Eerdmans, 2003.

Foerster, Werner. "ἔξεστιν." In *Theological Dictionary of the New Testament*, vol. 2, edited by Gerhard Kittel and Gerhard Friedrich, 561. Translated by Geoffrey W. Bromiley. Grand Rapids: Eerdmans, 1964–1976.

Gilbert, Maurice. *Ben Sira: Recueil d'études.* Leuven: Peeters, 2014.

Glancy, Jennifer A. *Slavery in Early Christianity.* Minneapolis: Fortress, 2006.

Ilan, Tal. *Integrating Women into Second Temple History.* Peabody: Hendrickson, 2001.

———. *Jewish Women in Greco-Roman Palestine.* Peabody: Hendrickson, 1996.

Instone-Brewer, David. *Divorce and Remarriage in the Bible: The Social and Literary Context.* Grand Rapids: Eerdmans, 2002.

Jackson, Bernard S., ed. *The Jewish Law Annual.* Vol. 4. Leiden: Brill, 1981.

Lövestam, Evald. "Divorce and Remarriage in the New Testament." In *The Jewish Law Annual*, Vol. 4, edited by Bernard S. Jackson, 47–65. Leiden: Brill, 1981.

Malina, Bruce J., and Richard L. Rohrbaugh. *Los evangelios sinópticos y la cultura mediterránea del siglo 1.* Navarra: Verbo Divino, 2002.

Martin, Dale B. "Slavery and Ancient Jewish Family." In *The Jewish Family in Antiquity*, edited by Shaye J. D. Cohen, 113–29. Atlanta: Scholars, 1993.

Moxnes, Halvor, ed. *Constructing Early Christian Families: Family as Social Reality and Metaphor.* London: Routledge, 1997.

———. *Poner a Jesús en su lugar: Una visión radical del grupo familiar y el Reino de Dios.* Navarra: Verbo Divino, 2005.

Neusner, Jacob. *The Mishnah: A New Translation.* New Haven: Yale University Press, 1988.

Núñez, Miguel. Solo por Gracia, "Miguel Núñez: El divorcio según la Biblia." YouTube. Accessed 17 September 2020. https://www.youtube.com/watch?v=vtoHKlYqlxw.

Ortega, Javier. *El Evangelio de Juan y la Iglesia (im)posible: Política eclesial a la luz de Juan 13–17.* Madrid: San Pablo, 2019.

Pellegrini, Silvia. "Mujeres sin nombre en los evangelios canónicos." In *Los Evangelios: Narraciones e historia*, edited by M. Navarro y M. Perroni, 393–432. Navarra: Verbo Divino, 2011.

Piper, John. Riquezas de Gracia, "¿Dios permite doble nupcias si hubo adulterio? John Piper." YouTube. 23 November 2018. Accessed 17 September 2020. https://www.youtube.com/watch?v=CUsWrn0PNtg.

Richter Raimer, Ivone. "'No temaís . . . id a ver . . . y anunciad': Mujeres en el Evangelio de Mateo." *Revista de Interpretación Bíblica Latinoamericana* 27 (1997): 145–61.

Saldarini, Anthony J. "Mujeres ausentes en los hogares de Mateo." In *Una compañera para Mateo*, edited by A. J. Levine, 247–65. Bilbao: Desclée de Brouwer, 2003.

Schüssler-Fiorenza, Elizabeth. "The Ethics of Biblical Interpretation: Decentering Biblical Scholarship." *Journal of Biblical Literature* 107 (1988): 3–17.

Vargas Machuca, A. "La llamada Fuente Q de los Evangelios Sinópticos." In *Fuentes del cristianismo: Tradiciones primitivas del sobre Jesús*, edited by Antonio Piñero, 63–94. Córdoba: El Almendro, 1993.

Wainwright, Elaine M. *Shall We Look for Another? A Feminist Rereading of the Matthean Jesus*. New York: Orbis, 1988.

6

The Church

A School for Double Citizenship

Ruth Padilla DeBorst

An Introductory Story

The nation was a prisoner to hyperinflation, an oppressive military dictatorship, and a war by the dictatorship as a smoke screen to cover up its crimes against humanity. Those who dared to question the repressive policies of the government were considered disloyal citizens who would be destined to "disappear." Even so, there was a lot of excitement in a small congregation one sunny March morning during the school year. It was "Ordination" day in the Baptist church on the outskirts of Buenos Aires. The boys and girls were the first: they ran up to the front and sat on the ground. The ministerial team, made up of women and men, laid their hands on the children. They told them, "So that you can grow well, learn, and be good friends with each other, and follow Jesus at home, at school, and in the neighborhood, we consecrate you." A resounding "Amen" rose up from the rest of the congregation. Next, the adolescents went up the front and made a colorful circle. They also received their charge. College students were the next ones to go forward. They were "ordained" to explore their vocations and to hone their skills for serving others. Workers and people in managerial positions, domestic workers, manual laborers, people in a wide variety of professions, campus pastors, members of the church pastoral staff, group by group, women and men, youth and senior citizens: all who were present were consecrated to live as citizens of God's kingdom within their specific occupations.

The occasion was celebrated with a classic Argentine meal, *empanadas* and grilled meat, in the church's patio area. After we had finished eating, we sat in a circle and began the community consultation. The question of the day was: Should we use wine or grape juice in the church's communion service? Historically, our church had always used wine in the Lord's Supper. Nevertheless, a recently arrived missionary had explained to the pastoral team that he could not participate in communion because he did not believe that Christians should drink alcohol. A frank and open conversation followed. "Why should we change our practice just because a North American missionary did not like the way we did things?" insisted many young adults. "But we should find ways to preserve our unity as the body of Christ – we cannot exclude any Christian from communion." "In addition," others asked, "what about those who are struggling with an addiction to drugs or alcohol? Wouldn't it be better for them if we didn't have alcohol in the church?" Younger and older people alike, women and men, freely expressed their points of view. The conversation then changed to address the need to recruit volunteers for the church's after-school ministry and the hiring of a social worker for the rehabilitation center sponsored by the church. And, from that day forward, half of the little cups in our communion service contained white grape juice, and the other half had red wine.

This chapter is not intended to prescribe what liquid is appropriate to fill communion cups, nor is it to pontificate about specific doctrines held by Baptists. What I do propose is that the church should be a school for double citizenship. On the one hand, the church is *apostolic*; it actively participates in the world by following Jesus through the power of the Spirit. On the other hand, it is *holy*, and it should question and never become too comfortable in the structures of an unequal, unjust, and violent world. It has precisely this double calling: to live in the world in the light of our identity as the people of the Triune Community-of-Love as both a *holy* and an *apostolic* community. This is what it means for the church to be a school of citizenship. The quality of the relationships, the values that are fleshed out, and the exercise of the gifts inside the community are training and practice for the family, work, and social relationships beyond the church.

These theological reflections about the church being holy and apostolic, and, therefore, a citizenship school, have been born from the dialogue that I have maintained between my reading of Scripture, my analysis of history, my experiences in a Baptist church in my formative years, and my participation in a variety of Christian faith communities throughout *Abya Yala* since then.[1]

---

1. The phrase *Abya Yala*, a word from the Guna indigenous group, means "land in full maturity" or "land of vital (life?) blood" and it designates the land that the Europeans called America. I use *Abya Yala* as preferable to "Latin America" because, as it refers to the land in

Ecclesial Citizenship in Practice

That Sunday in March on the outskirts of Buenos Aires, a quite unlikely group of people was gathered: "housewives," students, people in the process of overcoming drug or alcohol addiction, those who had been Christians "from birth" and others more recent in the faith, college graduates employed in a variety of fields, young people, manual laborers, immigrants, businesspeople, unemployed people, older adults, foreigners, and indigenous Argentines. Having experienced a long week of work and the strain of suffering under an oppressive government with a high cost of living, they found in our Sunday worship services an opportunity to rest and celebrate life with music and fellowship, to carry our personal and national burdens to God in prayer, to restore our hope through community reflection on the word of God, to battle through ethical dilemmas, and to gather courage to live faithfully through a new week.

Beyond this, for the majority of the people who were attending, the worship services and the assemblies were the only spaces where they could express their voices, where their opinions were well received and their perspectives were respectfully affirmed. Their annual service of "ordination" affirmed the lordship of Christ over every dimension of life and the value of each person – no one was more or less worthy than another – and each profession, because no task is more or less sacred than any other. Each person was recognized as an active member of the community and as a responsible citizen in God's economy. All were affirmed in their identity, dignity, and value as members of the people of God, with gifts granted by the Holy Spirit, and with a calling to follow Jesus in the world without fully belonging to that world. This was a real-life definition of the church, experienced less like a static condition and more like a constant movement in two directions. Jesus referred to this in his prayer for his disciples:

> My prayer is not that you take them out of the world but that you protect them from the evil one. They are not of the world, even as I am not of it. Sanctify them by the truth; your word is truth. As you sent me into the world, I have sent them into the world. (John 17:15–18)

This chapter proposes that the church be a school of double citizenship. On the one hand, the identity of the people of God is specific, distinctive, holy. On the other hand, these people are sent into the world in a radical following of Jesus to fulfill God's transformative, life-giving purposes. Without necessarily

---

itself, it does not make invisible the indigenous and African inhabitants and those from other backgrounds who live among the "Latinos."

articulating it in the words of the Nicene Creed, this double movement experienced by that local congregation echoed that ancient creed. In spite of the significant social and economic differences, they formed part of a new, holy community that had been brought together by God. That community was also an apostolic community, which was nurtured by the ministry of the apostles and sent into the world as a witness of the good news.

The Church, the Alternative People Invited by the Community-of-Love

What – or, better, who – is the church? Throughout history and in various contexts, this question has received quite varied conceptual answers and fleshed-out expressions. All of these rest on theological understandings of God's nature, human nature, and the relationship between them. This and the following section will explore these understandings.

The word "church" (*iglesia* in Spanish) is a translation of the Greek word *ekklesia*, a word that in the Greco-Roman context did not have a religious connotation. Neither did it refer to a physical place nor to an institutional structure. It referred to an assembly of citizens called to come out of their homes to gather in a public place to deal with "political" topics, that is, topics of interest shared by the inhabitants of the *polis* (community or city). When the Greeks governed the Mediterranean world, these assemblies had a certain decision-making power. Nevertheless, under the Roman Empire, these assemblies gradually lost their importance. They became opportunities for the emperor's heralds to announce the "gospel," the good news of the day. We will speak more about the good news below.

The writers of the testimonies and letters compiled in the Bible's New Testament took words in common use like *ekklesia* and infused them with a new and liberating meaning. Let's consider, for example, how Peter characterizes the community made up of followers of Jesus scattered throughout Asia Minor:

> But you are a chosen people, a royal priesthood, a holy nation, God's special possession, that you may declare the praises of him who called you out of darkness into his wonderful light. Once you were not a people, but now you are the people of God; once you had not received mercy, but now you have received mercy. (1 Pet 2:9–10)

Peter describes the church as a group whose dignity is granted by God's election and which has a religious identity (a royal priesthood) as well as a political one (nation and people). The church is composed of persons called to leave their particular circumstances in order to integrate into a new and distinct community. Different from the convocations in the *polis*, the call is not issued by some transient political authority, but rather by the sovereign Creator, who from long ago had already called out a people who would serve as a living expression of his good purposes in the world. In contrast to the precarious unity imposed by the Roman armies with their crucifixion deterrence, the church is attracted by the mercy of the incarnated, crucified, and resurrected Christ. Instead of finding themselves brought together out of a paralyzing fear and heavy taxes, the new community is woven together by the work of the life-giving Spirit who bridges the linguistic, ethnic, and social differences so that they might be the (one) people of God. To sum up, through God's action, the dispersed and varied Christians are transformed into the people of the Community-of-Love and citizens of a new kingdom. Citizenship under the government of this Community-of-Love cannot be bought or earned. It is not dependent on one's immigration status, nor the color of one's skin, nor one's ethnic background. To belong to the new humanity of God is freely granted to all people who admit their created condition, who recognize Jesus Christ as Savior and Lord, who are aware that their breath depends on the Spirit of life, who await God's complete restoration of all creation, and who live in the light of these confessions in the world.

Speaking biblically, citizenship under the sovereign Community-of-Love is not a spiritualized, otherworldly, or imaginary condition. It is a concrete "belongingness" that is embodied in the church. This community of flesh and blood is realistically described in the New Testament. As it grew and extended geographically, the early church faced cultural challenges, human greed, arguments over power, and external persecution. At the same time, they were learning how to navigate their own differences and nourish a perseverance filled with hope as they sang their faith, exchanged letters, and maintained their connections via trips and mutual visits. In spite of their growing pains and encounters with fallen human nature, the biblical and extrabiblical testimony of their contemporaries bears witness to the notable integrity between what was taught and what was practiced by those first Christians. In contrast to the opulent Greco-Roman temples, they did not spend money on buildings, as they gathered in their homes. The funds that were collected from the tithes and offerings were used to finance the trips of the itinerant pastors, to purchase freedom for slaves, and to take care of widows and orphans. Although it was a patriarchal society, women participated freely in the life of the community through their gifts, whether through hospitality, teaching, or the planting of new churches. When a city was suffering due to a plague and the inhabitants fled for their lives, the followers of Jesus moved into the city and took care of the sick. These communities distinguished themselves by their willingness to die for their faith, but never to kill for it.[2] In this way, the church grew because it practiced what it preached as an alternative community in which women and men, young people and older adults, slaves and free – without distinction of hierarchy – practiced a new citizenship for people's well-being, even for those who did not belong to the community.

The Church, a Community Sent into the World, Just Like Jesus

While the people of God are called to leave the world in order to constitute an alternative community, simultaneously they are called to enter into the world in fulfillment of God's original command to humanity and as a witness to the good news of the kingdom of God. We might ask, "What is that commandment?" And "What is the good news that the church witnesses to?"

The poetic song registered in Genesis 1 and 2 draws a picture of human beings created "in the image and likeness of God." This nature distinguishes them from the rest of the created order in two ways. First, human beings are the only ones able to recognize themselves as creatures and to establish a special bond with their Creator and among themselves. Created by the Community-of-Love, people fully live out their identity when they connect in love with this community, with other people, and with the rest of creation of which they are a part. Second, being created in God's image, the human community has been delegated to represent this Community-of-Love in the world. God entrusts to human beings – women and men – the creative tasks of being fruitful/multiplying and with love administrating the created order so that everything

---

2. See Alan Kreider, *La paciencia: El sorprendente fermento del cristianismo en el imperio romano*, BEB 156 (Salamanca: Sígueme, 2017); Rodney Stark, *La expansión del cristianismo: Un estudio sociológico* (Madrid: Trotta, 2009). The Epistle to Diognetus is an example of an ancient text that reveals the distinctive identity of the community composed of followers of Jesus: "For Christians are not distinguished from the rest of mankind either in locality or in speech or in customs. 2For they dwell not somewhere in cities of their own, neither do they use some different language, nor practise an extraordinary kind of life. 3Nor again do they possess any invention discovered by any intelligence or study of ingenious men, nor are they masters of any human dogma as some are. 4But while they dwell in cities of Greeks and barbarians as the lot of each is cast, and follow the native customs in dress and food and the other arrangements of life, yet the constitution of their own citizenship, which they set forth, is marvellous, and confessedly contradicts expectation. 5They dwell in their own countries, but only as sojourners; they bear their share in all things as citizens, and they endure all hardships as strangers. Every foreign country is a fatherland to them, and every fatherland is foreign." Diog. 5, Joseph Barber Lightfoot and J. R. Harmer, *The Apostolic Fathers* (London: Macmillan, 1891), 505–506.

might be good.³ Both dimensions of human nature are distorted by human rebellion: relationships are broken – they become unequal and oppressive – and tasks become a drudgery filled with pain.⁴ Even so, the good news is that God, sovereignly and lovingly, time and again takes the initiative to restore the relationship that provides identity and vocation to his people. God renews his covenant with all living beings and with his people for the well-being of the whole created order: that by means of a people who live according to God's good purposes, all the nations might be blessed.⁵ Through the Law and the Prophets, and in spite of the obstinacy of the people, God gradually and repeatedly reminds his people that, as such, they have received God's favor with a clear purpose. They are to have just relationships and to live in such a way that other people will come to know this good news.

In the climax of his loving action, God, the Supreme Creator Community, becomes human and shows historically what it means to be fully the "image and likeness" of God. Jesus Christ – the new Adam – incarnates the original healthy relationships and the original vocation of humanity and made known the good news of God's love in the midst of the false gospels of his day (Rom 5:12–13; 1 Cor 15:22).

Permit me to say again that the word "gospel" did not primarily have a religious connotation in the time of Jesus. It referred to what today we would call "the daily news." What constituted "gospel," or good news, for the emperor and his "lackies" was almost never good news for the people in general. If the "good news" was that the Roman army had expanded the borders of the empire, this would mean that the occupied people would have to pay higher taxes. More money would be needed to pay for larger armies to guard the borders and to build more roads to be traveled by those armies and more merchants selling their products. The Pax Romana was precariously maintained by nails

---

3. The Hebrew word *adam* means "human being." It should be distinguished from the proper name Adam, given to the male (*ish*) in contrast to Eve, who is the female (*isha*). According to the Genesis 2 narrative, in the midst of a good creation God recognized that "it is not good" for the man to be alone. Human beings, made in the image and likeness of God/Community, are community beings. See Catalina F. de Padilla and C. René Padilla, *Mujer y hombre en la misión de Dios* (Lima: Ediciones Puma, 2005).

4. God's words to the humans registered in Gen 3:14–19 are not a curse, but rather a description of the natural consequences of sin.

5. Notice that when God renews his covenant in the time of Noah, he does not renew it exclusively with Noah. Although this is suggested by the headings inserted by editors in many versions of the Bible, the covenant is made with "every living creature" (Gen 9:9–10). See the covenant that God made with Abraham in Gen 12:1–3.

and crosses, forced migration, and expropriation of land. The good news of the Roman Empire was not so good, after all!

In contrast to this caricature of gospel/good news, Jesus Christ fleshed out and made known the truly good news that God had not given up on humanity nor on his purposes for the well-being of the whole created order. The jaw-dropping and subversive good news is that God, the Sovereign Community, Creator, and Sustainer of all that exists, in Christ entered the world. In addition, far from entering through the magnificent gates of a Roman imperial family, with all the trappings of greatness and power, God came to a poor Palestinian woman and became a baby of the working class in an occupied territory, and he was visited by some simple shepherds. God became a vulnerable refugee in a foreign land. God became an anonymous laborer, working with stones and wood. God became an itinerant teacher, with no place to lay his head. God became a friend of a woman of ill repute, with ostracized foreigners, and with imperial lackies. God kneeled down to wash the dusty feet of perplexed fishermen and traitors. God became condemned as a criminal and was executed to show what would happen to anyone who dared to destabilize the deadly Pax Romana.

And from there, from down below, from the inside, God sovereignly brought about the most surprising reversal of all time. Upon entering this deepest darkness, the abyss of death, alienation, and absolute loneliness – Father, Father, why have you forsaken me? – God broke those chains of death, alienation, and absolute loneliness. The Community-of-Love leavened the dough of a fractured society with a true peace. In Christ, God continued the work of creation: he began to form a new humanity through the reconciling work of Jesus Christ. The Pax Christi wove together an improbable variety of women and men – slaves, slave owners, freed slaves, workers, rich landowners, Jews, and Greeks. In life and through his death and resurrection, Jesus Christ continued the work of restoring the relationships between humans and God, and at the same time, among human beings (2 Cor 5:19–20; Eph 2:14–15). This is how God continued his work of recreation: by repairing the broken relationships and by reestablishing the vocation of his people for the good of the entire creation. This is how God "moved into the neighborhood" (John 1:14 *The Message*). And in this same way, the Christian community is sent into the world.

The pattern of its involvement should reflect how Jesus interacted with that world. He is their King whom they represent. For the church, following Jesus demands a sacrificial incarnation in the midst of the disorder of the social, economic, political, and ecological realities. The goal is not to hobnob with the powerful, nor to acquire privileges, but rather to serve just as their Lord did. To adopt the lifestyle of Jesus is to favor people who have become marginalized by the systems of power and exclusion, to recruit them for an active ministry according to their gifts, and to restore them to a place of dignity within the church, the family, and society. To follow the King who chose the way of the cross and rejected violence implies, in the words of Orlando Costas, to abandon the projects of Christendom that confuse the kingdom of God with the institutional church, the gospel with the culture, and the power of the cross with the power of the sword.[6] To follow the King who rose from the dead and governs sovereignly today demands that we resist all forms of imperialism, that we relativize the authority of all men, governments, and powers, and that we pledge absolute allegiance to God alone. In the words of René Padilla, it requires that we "witness to God's purpose of love and justice revealed in Jesus Christ, in the power of the Holy Spirit."[7]

Double Citizenship

In summary, the essential identity of all people depends on their condition as beings created by the Community-of-Love, created in the image and likeness of this community. Given this nature, women and men are fully human when they live in harmonious relationships with their Creator, with other human beings, and with the rest of creation. They exercise their vocation when they fruitfully utilize the gifts given by the Spirit of life in favor of other people and in loving care of the planet that is our temporal home.

The people who assume this identity and exercise this vocation by the work and grace of the God-Community are both specific and distinctive and, at the same time, they are sent out to contribute to the common good as they follow Jesus Christ in the style modeled by Jesus Christ. The quality of the relationships, the values that are incarnated, and the exercise of gifts within this community are practice for the family, labor, and social relationships beyond the community. Ecclesial citizenship and belonging to the people of God under his reign shows the way to be citizens in the larger society.

---

6. Orlando E. Costas, *Christ outside the Gate: Mission beyond Christendom* (Maryknoll: Orbis, 1992), 181.

7. C. Rene Padilla, "The Ebb and Flow of Kingdom Theology and Its Implications for Missions," in *Evangelical and Frontier Mission Perspectives on the Global Progress of the Gospel*, ed. Beth Snodderly and A. Scott Moreau, ECB 9 (Oxford: Regnum, 2011), 285.

In conclusion, then, we will explore what should characterize the relationships among members of the church. What should be the values demonstrated by the community that follows Jesus? Who exercises gifts in this community and which gifts are they?

The Good News of Relationships Restored by Jesus Christ

The poetic narrative of Genesis describes the man and the woman as beings created equally in the image and likeness of God and therefore sharing the same status, dignity, and value. The man (*ish* in Hebrew) recognized the woman (*isha*) as his equal. He rejoices because he finds in her what he did not find in any animal: a faithful partner. It is only with the fall, described in Genesis 3, that the relationships become distorted. Suffering and domination enter the scenario, as deadly consequences of the human rebellion. The good news of the reign of Jesus Christ is that these distorted relationships can be restored to their original egalitarian quality. While the cultures of the Near East were profoundly patriarchal, it is notable that the Scriptures give significant space to women in protagonist roles, and many of them were foreigners. In contrast to custom, in Jesus's genealogy women are listed (Tamar, Rahab, Ruth, and Bathsheba). Among his friends and followers were various women (Mary the mother of James and Joseph, Mary Magdalene, Salome, Susanna, Mary, and Martha, among others). There were women who stood at the foot of the cross while almost all the male disciples fled; and these women were the first witnesses of the resurrection.

In his teaching to the early Christian communities, Paul emphasizes the restoration brought about by Jesus Christ. Thanks to Jesus, "there is neither Jew nor Gentile, neither slave nor free, nor is there male and female, for you are all one in Christ Jesus" (Gal 3:28). This conviction moves the apostle to subvert a custom rooted in his time. It was customary to circulate letters with ethical advice. These included domestic codes, that is, advice about how to live, with some very precise rules to preserve the social order. What was unusual in the Ephesian code (5:21–33) was that Paul did not only prescribe appropriate conduct for women, children, and slaves. Traditionally, these persons were exhorted to submit to the powerful men, fathers, and slave owners. Paul dared to demand mutual submission by all persons in the new community of equals that had been inaugurated by Jesus Christ.

Abya Yala is known for being the region with the greatest number of violent acts committed against women, and our countries are plagued by femicides. Abuse and objectification of women and girls have become commonplace, even in our churches. Our communities of faith must subvert the established order and we must resist every form of machismo and discrimination. We must also affirm, through word and deed, that women and men share citizenship as equals under the reign of Jesus Christ.

The Good News of the Values of God's Kingdom

The people of God are portrayed biblically as that people who demonstrate, in flesh and blood, God's good purposes in the midst of human history. Being subject to and praising God should be manifested in daily ethics. The old law detailed the economic and social parameters that would distinguish this people from others. The prophets warned the people when they strayed from the path of justice, equity, and providing for all people, including foreigners. Centuries later, Jesus inserted himself in that same prophetic role and took upon himself the passage of Isaiah 61, known in the synagogue in Nazareth, as his ministerial priorities (Luke 4:18–19). At the same time – and this is what greatly irritated his hearers – he went way beyond the passage, because he refused to take up the role of avenger. To the contrary, he emphasized God's grace for all people.[8]

In the midst of the imperialistic pretensions of Rome – with its colonialist violence and the concomitant economic and social inequality – and the self-gratifying accommodation of the Jewish religious and political leaders – who manipulated the law for their own benefit – Jesus incarnates and promotes a totally alternative system of values. He is the Master who kneels to wash the feet of his disciples. He is the King who does not have anywhere to lay his head. He is the Lord who gives himself for others. At the same time, his teaching, and especially that compiled in the Sermon on the Mount, details the ethical expectations that should characterize the people of God.

When in our Latin American countries the number of people who identify as evangelical Protestants grows, but at the same time violence, inequality, poverty, and the abuse of creation also grow, it forces us to analyze what kinds of values we are nurturing in our faith communities. Who do the church leaders serve? Are our congregations places of inclusion and welcome? Is our defense of life holistic? That is, are we concerned about the life conditions of people who are alive, or just about fetuses or those who have already died? As Walter Brueggemann says:

---

8. In his reading of Isa 61, Jesus did not read "and the day of vengeance of our God" (v. 2).

For ethics in the world and for the shape of humane and generative public policy, homework must be ecclesial. That is, good public policy requires the formation and nurture of sub-communities of courage and passion that are about the daily business of praise and obedience, that are devoted to the will of God, meditating on it day and night, and that actively await the full and soon coming of God's governance.[9]

An ecclesial citizenship that identifies and nurtures the values of God's kingdom and his justice is a prerequisite for a responsible citizenship in a wider context. Without these, the political involvement of Christians will be nothing more than reflecting the world's values and will not reflect God's purposes.

The Good News of the Gifts of the Spirit

Neither following Jesus nor living out the values of God's kingdom is possible without the action of the Holy Spirit. As a member of the Community-of-Love, the Spirit is the one who since creation and throughout history inspires life and gives to the entire people of God the wisdom and the gifts needed to live as God desires.

In the Greco-Roman *polis*, full citizenship (with voice and vote) was limited to men, and only those with economic resources. In the Jewish religious system, women were relegated to a second level. The New Testament paints a quite different picture. In Peter's speech on the day of Pentecost, the apostle quoted the old prophecy of Joel as an explanation for what was occurring in the early church:

> In the last days, God says,
> I will pour out my Spirit on all people.
> Your sons and daughters will prophesy,
> your young men will see visions,
> your old men will dream dreams.
> Even on my servants, both men and women,
> I will pour out my Spirit in those days,
> and they will prophesy. (Acts 2:17–18)

In the early community of followers of Jesus Christ, the ministry of women and men was determined by the gifts that each person (male or female) had

---

9. Walter Brueggemann, "Vision for a New Church and a New Century: Holiness Become Generosity," *Union Seminary Quarterly Review* 54, no. 1–2 (2000): 45.

received from the Spirit. The male apostles are well known. But it is important to recognize the leadership that women exercised. Priscilla is identified as a partner and exercised a pastoral and educational role, together with her husband (Acts 18 and elsewhere). As a deaconess, Phoebe supported the ministry of Paul and of others (Rom 16:1–2). Tabitha (Dorcas) ministered to the needy (Acts 9:36). Lydia hosted Paul and Silas in her home (Acts 16). Phillip's daughters prophesied (Acts 21:9). Paul identified Junia as an "apostle" (Rom 16:7). Euodia and Syntyche are mentioned as women who had "contended" side by side with Paul in "the cause of the gospel" (Phil 4:2–3). The variety of ministries exercised by these women demonstrates that the early church made a great effort to overcome the patriarchal customs of the Jewish and Greco-Roman environments around them as they followed their Master.

Conclusion: Examples and Questions

Renewed relationships, alternative values, a reassignment of roles based on gifts: all of these are processes that require the exercise of the double citizenship in our faith communities and are nourished by it. This provides an integral witness to the good news of God's kingdom in our context. Samuel Escobar says that the Protestant/evangelical/Pentecostal churches have "become alternative societies that create a closed world where people are accepted and become actors, not on the basis of what gives them status in the world around but of values that come from their vision of the kingdom of God."[10]

In a similar vein, and having researched a variety of churches in Central America, a Catholic sociologist highlights some Protestant congregations in El Salvador. Although "individualized rituals of community building such as prayer, Bible reading for personal application, and personal testimony" could be considered socially alienating, they serve as "micro acts of democracy." He continues:

> Over time, perhaps even over generations, what begins in conversion and is sustained in the context of such deeply rooted communities of faith and personal piety, could lead to the kinds of social organization that have the power to rise up against injustice, overturn the submissive status quo politics of

---

10. Samuel Escobar, "A Missiological Approach to Latin American Protestantism," *International Review of Mission* 87, no. 345 (1998): 170.

traditional Christianity, and lay down foundations for democratic participation and social change.[11]

The narrative about that March day in Buenos Aires illustrates these processes. Belonging to an ecclesial community serves as practice for citizenship in the larger society. Faced with this, we close with some necessary questions in light of these reflections. Is the evangelical Protestant church, at a country level within Latin America and in the rest of the world, living out its calling as a people called to leave the world and to adopt its identity and primary vocation as the people of the Community-of-Love? Is their community life such that all of the members participate as active citizens and are consecrated and sent out to contribute as Christians in the wider society? Are the presence and witness of the church in the world distinctive, not as a result of some decorative religiosity but rather due to its ethical incarnation of God's kingdom and justice? Does the church pledge absolute allegiance to the powers of the day or to the Lord of life, the God of history?

The people who were gathered that March morning were being educated in these issues. As they faced the world in the light of the Word, and vice versa, they were growing in their ability to live out a different kind of citizenship as active members of the reign of the Community-of-Love in their families, in their neighborhoods, in their jobs, and in society. Through the grace of God and the work of the Holy Spirit, may that take place in all the communities of Jesus followers in our beloved *Abya Yala*!

References

Brueggemann, Walter. "Vision for a New Church and a New Century: Holiness Become Generosity." *Union Seminary Quarterly Review* 54, no. 1–2 (2000): 45–64.

Costas, Orlando E. *Christ outside the Gate: Mission beyond Christendom.* Maryknoll: Orbis, 1992.

Escobar, Samuel. "A Missiological Approach to Latin American Protestantism." *International Review of Mission* 87, no. 345 (1998): 161–73.

Kreider, Alan. *La paciencia: El sorprendente fermento del cristianismo en el imperio romano.* BEB 156. Salamanca: Sígueme, 2017.

Padilla, Catalina F. de, and C. René Padilla. *Mujer y hombre en la misión de Dios.* Lima: Ediciones Puma, 2005.

---

11. Timothy Wadkins, "Getting Saved in El Salvador: The Preferential Option for the Poor," *International Review of Mission* 97, no. 384–385 (2008): 46.

Padilla, C. René. "The Ebb and Flow of Kingdom Theology and Its Implications for Missions." In *Evangelical and Frontier Mission Perspectives on the Global Progress of the Gospel*, edited by Beth Snodderly and A. Scott Moreau, 274–285. ECB 9. Oxford: Regnum, 2011.

Stark, Rodney. *La expansión del cristianismo: Un estudio sociológico*. Madrid: Trotta, 2009.

Wadkins, Timothy. "Getting Saved in El Salvador: The Preferential Option for the Poor." *International Review of Mission* 97, no. 384–385 (2008): 31–49.

7

A Crisis in Latin American Evangelical Leadership

Between Intolerance and Incongruity

Dinorah B. Méndez

It is possible to find secular studies that address the topic of Latin American culture in general, and even its religious characteristics, although these are usually addressed from a sociological point of view. It is more difficult to find religious research that analyzes Latin American cultures or societies from theological or ethical perspectives, and fewer still are the studies that bring together relations between these cultures and their interactions with evangelical[1] churches. This chapter concentrates specifically on an analysis of important characteristics in leadership concepts and conduct whose common thread is Latin American culture, with special reference to the author's context.

---

1. The term "evangelical" is used in this chapter in a specific way, as is the term "Protestant" to identify non-Catholics. See Donald P. Hustad, ¡Regocijaos! La Música Cristiana en la Adoración (El Paso: Casa Bautista de Publicaciones, 1998), 14–18. This author applies the term "evangelical" to several Christian denominations, including Pentecostals. In his view the perception of the term has changed over time. However, from the Reformation in the sixteenth century, Protestants were considered evangelicals. Later the meaning of "evangelical" was "conservative" in rejection of the liberal theology of the nineteenth century. In one sense, the evangelicals in Latin America are a trend among the main Protestant denominations. Therefore, the term "evangelical" is used in this study in reference to all Protestant groups, without taking into consideration the denominational differences. See Pablo A. Deiros, Protestantismo en América Latina (Nashville: Editorial Caribe, 1997), 39–50; see also Samuel Escobar, "Interpretations of Popular Protestantism," in New Face of the Church in Latin America, ed. Guillermo Cook (Maryknoll: Orbis, 1994), 114–16; Dinorah B. Méndez, Evangelicals in México: Their Hymnody and Its Theology (Brussels: Peter Lang, 2008), 95–96.

The main purpose is to evaluate current leadership in Protestant churches. Do leaders manifest more the influence of these cultural characteristics which contrast with the biblical model of the servant leader, whose prime example is Jesus? Or has there been biblical influence in the concepts and practices of leadership that can be perceived in the dominant sociocultural context in the prevalent religiosity in Latin America? Or, more precisely, what is the context of the author's homeland, Mexico?

Leadership Characteristics in the Latin American Socioreligious Context

The phenomenon of religion has been studied in our continent, not only of the majority church (Catholicism) as an institution, but also in the consciousness of individual Catholics. This has covered many areas of life, including economic and political aspects. Popular grassroots Catholicism in Latin America has a syncretical strand which brings into the religious consciousness some aspects of indigenous polytheisms. All of this has led to the appearance of messianic leadership styles, in both political and religious spheres.[2] It is interesting to analyze why so many people in our continent, instead of venerating sacred images, worship people of flesh and blood, generally men. These are their political bosses, their quintessential bosses, *caudillo* bosses. They might be priests or *holy* men. Some sociologists and anthropologists consider that this type of messianic and revolutionary phenomenon happens in societies like that of Latin America because education has been greatly influenced by religion and faith. It is seen in all fields of human thought, such as cultural, social, and political aspects.[3]

The main model of evangelical church leadership structures in Latin America, which was introduced by missionaries in the nineteenth century, was mostly democratic or congregational. This was demonstrated when an invitation was made to an individual's free will to accept Christ and then be baptized. Believers were given the opportunity to express their opinions and actively participate in their churches. They did not have these freedoms in other spheres of society. Nevertheless, this model was not, and has not been, consistently applied in all places. The principal problem is that this democratic model was in conflict with the Latin American cultural reality

---

2. Jacque Lafaye, *Mesías, cruzadas, utopías: El judeo-cristianismo en las sociedades iberoamericanas* (Mexico: FCE, 1997), 8–9.

3. Lafaye, *Mesías, cruzadas, utopías*, 10.

shaped by a colonial mentality – that is, a Catholic authoritarianism and a hierarchical society. This confirms the trend toward an authoritarian leadership that minimizes the participation of other people. This is certainly a doctrinal deficiency, but it is also contextual, where leadership exercised by the congregation has been restricted or even eliminated.[4]

It can be said, therefore, that one characteristic of leadership in Latin American culture is that, in many cases, leaders are seen as gods, demigods, or at the very least, as supernatural or messianic figures. These leaders, especially if they have dictatorial tendencies, try to demonstrate spectacular signs for their followers, and if they become martyrs, with even greater impetus the people consider them to be "saints." This, Jacque Lafaye states, shows that in Latin America belief and faith are more important than ideas and doctrines; that is to say, "religion is prior to ideology."[5] In other words, for this topic of leadership, it seems that Latin American people are not so much guided by principles or doctrine as mesmerized by a "messianic-caudillo."[6]

On the other hand, given the nature of a syncretistic religion, Catholicism has lost credibility over time. It is considered by a large number of Latin Americans to be a nominal religion that does not provide adequate, relevant answers for our lived reality. It is seen as a superficial, inconsistent religiosity in which what is believed in theory about morality and religion is not lived out in practice. That is to say, in the Latin American socioreligious context, there is an inconsistency between what is preached and what is practiced, an incongruent morality that, of course, is reflected in other aspects of leadership.[7]

Cultural Influence in Evangelical Leadership

In this section we will analyze some concepts that are based not primarily on evangelical convictions, but rather on the socioreligious background of the continent. This emerged from research that I conducted through the use of surveys of pastors, leaders, and other members of Baptist churches who attended the annual meetings of the Mexican National Baptist Convention.

---

4. Dinorah B. Méndez, "La misión de los evangélicos en el México actual," in *Reformulando la misión en Latinoamérica*, eds. Míguel Álvarez and Dinorah B. Méndez (Mexico: CUPSA, 2019), 178–79.

5. Lafaye, *Mesías, cruzadas, utopías*, 18.

6. Lafaye, 25.

7. Dinorah B. Méndez, "La esfera socio-religiosa de la cultura mexicana y su influencia en la teología y práctica de las iglesias bautistas de México" (diss., Seminario Teológico Bautista de México, 1989), 60–64.

Although I conducted these surveys decades ago, Mexico's sociocultural reality has not changed very much since then, and the reality of the churches even less. Changes that have taken place in society – such as respect for the rights of women – have not even been considered in our churches as worthy to be discussed. Therefore, as the author of this research and of this chapter, I consider that the data and implications continue to be valid and very pertinent today. The results of that research appear in my thesis cited in the footnotes.[8] The following comments come from that research but are limited to the topic of leadership.

As we analyze the concept of the pastor, the concepts of God and holiness are also involved. The following data emerged from the surveys: more than 60 percent believed that the pastor was holier than other Christians. More than 50 percent in each region (northern, central, and southern Mexico) knew members who believed that a pastor's prayers were more effective than other Christians' prayers. Finally, regarding whether they would accept non-ordained persons preaching in their church, around 20 percent said they would not accept them under any circumstances. About 40 percent said they would accept such a person, but only if certain requirements were met, such as the person having a good testimony and having been trained to preach, having been "called" to preach, or having had a specific church authorize the person to preach. I consider this percentage of people who thought it was right to let others preach according to biblical criteria to be relatively low. This result indicates that the concept of the pastor is influenced greatly by the culture, and by the dominant Catholic religion with its ideas of "priesthood" and of a certain hierarchy or "difference" between the group consecrated to the service of the Lord (the clergy) and the rest of the congregation (the laity).

The above information is reinforced with data regarding the opinions that the survey provided regarding women preaching from the pulpit. It is clear that when reference was made specifically to women, the numbers of negative opinions increased. What is curious is that many who affirmed that they were in favor of women preaching also considered that the spiritual gifts are given without distinction of gender. They also believed that in Christ we are all equal and in the priesthood of all believers. Nevertheless, regarding the use of the pulpit, in their opinion it was not true that we are equal. Regarding this question, they answered "no," that is, we are all equal and women can preach . . . but they should not use the pulpit to do so. In this section, as we

---

8. Méndez, "La esfera socio-religiosa," 121–29. The following section comes principally from material developed in the research that was quoted.

consider the concept of worship, and by necessity the concept of holiness, we see the influence of Roman Catholic ideas which affirm that the altar is sacred, in the sense that ordinary Christians cannot and should not approach it; only those who are "authorized" can do so. It seems that what the Bible teaches about holiness is not clear in their minds, and they are shaped more by popular Catholic ideas that circulate among the population.

To reaffirm the above, we now present the results of the survey regarding the direct influences of culture. A considerable number of respondents saw culture as negative and restricting the gospel. They even admitted that evangelicals themselves had transmitted some negative traditions. It is interesting to note that some specific Catholic practices are evident in the lives of evangelicals due to "Sunday-only Christians" who are not committed to the tasks of the church, nor totally given over to the Lord. They are irresponsible and passive in the church, content to "recite a prayer" or "to give alms." These evangelicals celebrate Catholic activities around Christmas and Holy Week, mourning practices, candles for the dead, and, in some places, services for the dead, with the body present. Another category includes concepts of hierarchy and "priestliness" regarding the pastor and the laity. They also include ideas of "holiness" and "reverence" in the sanctuary, that is, the church building. At other times they see the ordinances (baptism and the Lord's Supper) and prayers as a type of rite or sacrament. Another kind of influence is to follow the same social lifestyle and the same superstitions and customs. They do not manifest a change in lifestyle that is different from the world that surrounds us. Some evangelical churches and believers practice vestiges of Catholic kermesses. On the other hand, although to a lesser degree, they have received certain doctrinal, and, more importantly, ethical concepts. Evangelicals have accepted Catholic arguments regarding abortion and family planning. And if they do not accept these ideas, at least they don't disagree in public. Another aspect of cultural influence is seen in the type of worship service which generally is practiced passively with only a few participants up the front, who direct the service in a very formal and classical way.

The analysis presented here is necessarily incomplete. Readers who are interested in these topics can pursue them further. It is also important to recognize that societies in our continent are going through constant change and will become increasingly pluralistic, exposed to all kinds of ideological influences. In the future, when one wants to analyze these aspects of Protestant life or others, it will be necessary to take into consideration the kind of world we are living in.

Evangelical Leadership as Good News

The previous pages have offered a brief and limited review of the characteristics of Latin American society in one of its sectors, the phenomenon of leadership. This review does not claim to have been complete and exhaustive, but it does provide a panorama that is sufficient for understanding the context and, specifically, its interaction with evangelical life today.

In light of what has been presented, the influence of culture on evangelical churches seems undeniable. Faced with this fact, at least three different postures can be assumed. The first would be to reject the evidence and ignore it, like an ostrich that believes that by burying its head in the sand the threat is ended. This is a posture of indifference; that is, if we don't acknowledge culture's influence, it will go away. The consequence of this first option is that culture will continue to have influence, but with the disadvantage that we will not be aware of it. It can influence evangelical life without being examined or evaluated. We will not be able to keep that which is good and reject the bad aspects of that cultural impact.

The second option is to take the posture that, given the immensity of the cultural impact, and recognizing the magnitude of the task to counteract that impact or even understand it, evangelicals should opt for the path of retreat. They should isolate themselves as much as possible from the world that surrounds them and strive to avoid contact with the culture. However, such isolation would be relative, or even impossible, unless they moved to a remote mountain or some other place away from society. And even if this minimal contact with society were possible, the church of Jesus Christ would not then fulfill its task of being present in the community to give a powerful witness to eternal truths. This posture would make fulfilling the Great Commission impossible.

Finally, there is a third possibility, which is to acknowledge the reality of cultural influence from the world in which we live. The idea behind this option is to have our feet planted firmly on the ground and to evaluate the world that surrounds us. We can then admit that this world impacts all social groups and that such impact has both positive and negative aspects. As a consequence, this posture would result in a different series of attitudes among evangelicals. They would need to be alert to cultural influences and discern which aspects are compatible with Christian values, and when acquired, would redound to the fulfillment of the Lord's eternal purposes. At the same time, every congregation should educate itself so as to be prepared to detect and reject those cultural aspects which, when implemented, tend to weaken the gospel and block the witness and message that we Christians have been entrusted with.

Conclusions

This chapter ends by opening the door with an invitation for others to do better and additional research on the interesting topic of culture and the particularities of it that evangelicals manifest. The perspectives that this research opens are as follows:

In the first place, the lack of literature exploring these themes indicates the need for evangelicals to be more open regarding the world that surrounds them. This means not closing themselves off in their own world, because, as we have mentioned, such isolation leads to not fulfilling the task of being witnesses to the Lord Jesus Christ. By being open they will not lose their distinctiveness as New Testament Christians. On the contrary, fulfilling that task requires being interested in the world and the culture in which Protestants live, so that they will know and use better strategies to present the gospel. This involves translating the eternal truths into terms that are understandable to their neighbors.

In the second place, evangelicals need to open their eyes to the need for some of their members to become interested in social or contextual theology and dedicate themselves to studying it. This means, on the one hand, analyzing the society in which they live to observe its needs, and on the other hand, living out an integral gospel that describes and defines them. These two characteristics would have the specific goal of impacting society with greater effectiveness through the truths of the gospel. These need to be expressed in significant ways for the society and culture, with the ultimate goal of being better disciples and better makers of disciples of Christ.

Finally, while doing my research (and studying that of others), I acquired a deep personal sadness that many evangelicals claim to have a distinctive faith, yet have lives quite similar to those of their Catholic neighbors. There is very little difference in conduct, ethics, beliefs, or ideas. They continue to be Mexicans heavily shaped by the culture in which they live. It seems that the gospel has entered their minds but not their lives. As the author of this chapter, it is my desire that what I write be useful not only to evangelicals leaders, but also to a large segment of the church's members. My hope is that they may reflect upon our situation and remedy it.

It is terrible that our Latin America is so apathetic that, while our countries have such advanced and just laws, they exist only on paper. Our reality involves widespread corruption. The same thing has happened among many evangelicals. Our doctrine is good and lines up with the New Testament, but our lives are just like those of our neighbors, whether they identify themselves as religious or as nonbelievers.

This chapter is an invitation to reflection and change. Our end goal is to have a theology that is grounded in the Scriptures and in an all-powerful God who reveals himself in cultures and transcends them. A special challenge is for our church leaders to overcome the crisis of credibility. This crisis exists due to the lack of ethical consistency and integrity between our beliefs and our practices. At the same time, there is a need to resist the dominant cultural model of leadership, which is authoritarian, hierarchical, and intolerant. That understanding of leadership is incompatible with the servant-leadership modeled by our Lord and Teacher, Jesus Christ.

Finally, it is my wish that, upon finishing reading this chapter, readers will have a sense of total consecration to the Lord, always seeking to give honor and glory to him, who is the only one who is worthy. Amen.

References

Deiros, Pablo A. *Protestantismo en América Latina*. Nashville: Editorial Caribe, 1997.

Escobar, Samuel. "Interpretations of Popular Protestantism." In *New Face of the Church in Latin America*, edited by Guillermo Cook, 161–73. Maryknoll: Orbis, 1994.

Hustad, Donald P. *¡Regocijaos! La Música Cristiana en la Adoración*. El Paso: Casa Bautista de Publicaciones, 1998.

Lafaye, Jacque. *Mesías, cruzadas, utopías: El judeo-cristianismo en las sociedades iberoamericanas*. Mexico: FCE, 1997.

Méndez, Dinorah B. "La esfera socio-religiosa de la cultura mexicana y su influencia en la teología y práctica de las iglesias bautistas de México." Diss., Seminario Teológico Bautista de México, 1989.

———. *Evangelicals in México: Their Hymnody and Its Theology*. Brussels: Peter Lang, 2008.

———. "La misión de los evangélicos en el México actual." In *Reformulando la misión en Latinoamérica*, edited by Míguel Álvarez and Dinorah B. Méndez, 173–86. Mexico: CUPSA, 2019.

8

Protestants, Democracy, and Citizenship

Darío López

There is an undeniable fact of our current reality that has captured the attention of the mass media, political analysts, and observers of Latin American religion. A segment of Latin American Protestants, with very few aspects of democracy, has made an unexpected, previously unthinkable, and surprising incursion into the political arena. This public space requires democratic principles such as respect, dialogue, and tolerance.

This sector of Protestant churches does not understand that public policies are born from dialogue, negotiated compromises, and agreements between diverse actors of civil society and the political community. In addition, it considers that its religious vision of life must be accepted by all citizens, believers and unbelievers alike. They think that public policies need to bear their specific religious brand and not take into account the opinions of those who might have a different perspective.

Traditional Protestant Political Abstentionism

Years ago, when it was believed that religion was to be limited to one's personal life and separated from political day-to-day realities, it was unthinkable that undemocratic Protestants would enter the political arena. The reason was the following:

> Traditionally, Protestants in Latin America (as in many other places around the world) have considered ourselves "apolitical." We have considered "politics to be dirty" and we have quite openly

taken refuge in an individualistic, otherworldly Christianity. After all, "didn't Jesus say that his kingdom was not of this world?"[1]

This situation has changed. The Protestants who had little experience of democracy, who were traditionally apolitical, and who opposed involvement in politics, to the surprise of many moved their pulpits into the streets. Their religious discourse which had been confined to the four walls of their church buildings now entered the political arena. They are now in the public plaza! Nevertheless, when we examine this new situation, we must not omit a fact of reality:

> Many evangelicals who enter politics are not members of churches or groups that have always expressed interest in political life – the most traditional (mainline?) churches, frequently and critically called "liberal" – but rather members of churches for whom politics was always considered with suspicion, not helpful for Christians, and perhaps even a slippery slope, and, frankly, diabolical. These Christians who used to blatantly affirm "A Christian should not get involved in politics" are those (or their children) who have produced this political involvement by Protestants.[2]

So what happened? Did those Protestants who used to be apolitical and opposed to politics change their theology and become convinced that social and political actions are legitimate dimensions of their Christian testimony? One way to respond to this question is to affirm that the presence of a non/democratic sector of Protestant churches is related to the return of religion to the public arena in contemporary societies, especially regarding the growing number of debates around public policies.

When we observe what is happening in various countries of Latin America and the Caribbean, it is a fact of our reality that a sector of non/democratic Protestant churches has been – and continues to be – a visible, polemical, and key actor in electoral processes. Their vote and public support, favoring candidates who promised to defend the "traditional family," was very important in elections in the region. This could be seen in the elections in Guatemala when Jimmy Morales was elected president; in Honduras with the election of Juan Hernández; in Brazil when the far-right presidential candidate Jair

---

1. C. René Padilla, *Discipulado y misión: Compromiso con el Reino de Dios* (Buenos Aires: Kairós, 1997), 135.

2. José Míguez Bonino, *Poder del evangelio y poder político: La participación de los evangélicos en la política de América Latina* (Buenos Aires: Kairós, 1999), 12.

Bolsonaro was elected; and in Costa Rica when Fabricio Alvarado was almost elected to the presidency.

Protestants, Society, and Politics: A Panoramic Vision

Ever since their missionary insertion toward the end of the nineteenth century and the beginning of the twentieth century, and given their condition as a religious minority in a largely Roman Catholic continent, Protestant missionaries felt obligated to be involved in politics. They formed alliances with liberal, anticlerical political sectors in order to achieve democratic rights, such as freedom of religion, civil marriage, secular cemeteries, and access to education for women. This explains why the missionary acts of the first Protestant churches needed to be accompanied by social and political acts, with the goal of guaranteeing their presence in Latin American countries.

The first and most progressive missions and churches were open to the construction of democracies because they wanted a greater presence and involvement of Protestants in public life. They had a special interest in areas that were essential for democracy, such as public education and health. This was necessary because missionary work that was more open to public life, and not limited to private life, favored freedom of action for religious denominations that were not Roman Catholic.[3]

Nevertheless, the presence of Protestant churches in public life changed significantly from about 1945, when politically and theologically more conservative missions started to arrive, principally from the United States. The theological-political orientation of these missions ideologically dominated the majority of the Protestant churches in Latin America. This reduced missionary work to activity directed toward numerical church growth and the planting of new congregations. As a result, Protestants abandoned their concern for public issues. The gospel became understood as a truth oriented toward life's private spaces, a truth that required a retreat from the world, a message restricted to inside church buildings, and a religious discourse for souls without bodies.

There are, therefore, various reasons that explain this apolitical dimension that, traditionally, has characterized a large sector of Latin American and Caribbean Protestants:

---

3. Juan Fonseca, *Misioneros y Civilizadores: Protestantismo y modernización en el Perú (1915–1930)* (Lima: Fondo Editorial de la Pontificia Universidad Católica del Perú, 2002); Carlos Mondragón, *Leudar la masa: El pensamiento social de los protestantes en América Latina: 1920–1950* (Buenos Aires: Kairós, 2005).

(1) The influence of missionaries whose teaching (perhaps due more to what they were than what they taught) completely ignored the social and political responsibility of Christians. . . . (2) The Protestant "minority complex," set within a hostile environment (and sometimes open religious persecution), an environment where the issue of one's own survival has displaced all questions that could be raised about a possible contribution to the building of a new society. . . . (3) The emphasis on a futuristic eschatology in Protestant churches, in which social and political actions are identified as tasks that are foreign to the interests of Christians.[4]

It became necessary to understand the gospel as a public truth, as a truth that questions and exposes personal and structural sins, as the word that dignifies cultures, and as the word that produces social transformation.

A Change of Mind?

Did Latin American Protestants, who during the previous decades had been unconcerned about democracy, have a change of mind regarding politics which traditionally they had considered to be "worldly" and improper for believers to be engaged in? This is not really what has happened. They are not (really) interested in democracy, the common good, or social justice. Their real interest is to make a foray into public policies and, over the medium term, to capture and take over the State in order to install a theocracy. Their political-religious interest does not strive to strengthen democracy nor to construct a nation of equals. Among many reasons, they believe that public policies (health care, sexuality, population, and education) must be subordinated to religious beliefs and should be based on religious convictions.[5] In other words, the "incursion of the 'political Protestants' responds more to a new logic of the instrumental utilization of politics with religious goals rather than a historical utilization of religion for political ends."[6]

---

4. C. René Padilla, "Los evangélicos: Nuevos actores en el escenario político latinoamericano," in *De la marginación al compromiso: Los evangélicos y la política en América Latina*, ed. C. René Padilla (Buenos Aires: Fraternidad Teológica Latinoamericana, 1991), 5.

5. Darío López, "Protestantismo y espiritualidad en América Latina," in *¿Hacia dónde va el Protestantismo en América Latina?*, eds. H. Fernando Bullón and Nicolás Panotto (Buenos Aires: Kairós, 2017), 166.

6. José Luis Pérez Guadalupe and Sebastián Grundberger, eds., *Evangélicos y poder en América Latina* (Lima: Instituto de Estudios Social Cristianos-Konrad Adenauer Stiftung, 2018), 95.

The Contemporary Social and Political Context

There are three reasons that can explain the surge of new collective actors, such as Protestants, on the Latin American and Caribbean political scene. The three reasons are related to the fractures that have occurred in the political life of the countries in the region, with the breakdown of the traditional system of political parties.

In the first place, there is a growing disillusionment and loss of credibility in traditional politicians. In recent years, their most visible characteristics have been corruption scandals, peddling influence, and interference in other agencies and institutions of the State with the goal of politically controlling them.

In the second place, the crisis in the party system is evident. This is most obvious in democratic instability and in the poor training of political cadres for the exercise of power. The absence of training of party politicians results in a poverty of political debate, an inability to propose public policies oriented toward the common good, and a lack of independence to act according to one's conscience instead of according to party interests.

In the third place, we see an increase in the number of "outsiders." These are people who are outside the political community, with no political training, without a political party, and who are novices in the exercise of power. For the purposes of democracy, the presence of these "outsiders" has had a pernicious effect, as has been the case in Peru. They emerged in a specific moment with the goal of winning an election, but they were not prepared to represent, legislate, or govern adequately, and they did not have a national program.[7]

The Religious-Theological Context

The religious-theological reasons that explain the unexpected interest in public issues by Protestants with little experience of democracy are the following:

First, there has been an accelerated numerical growth in Protestant churches that could provide a significant voting bloc in election processes. For those Protestants with little background in democracy, this quantitative growth is interpreted as a sign of divine approval. The "children of God"

---

7. The Peruvian case is quite illustrative: (1) An ex-president (Alberto Fujimori) was sent to prison for crimes against humanity. Recently he was pardoned for reasons that are unclear but was again ordered back to prison. (2) Another ex-president (Alejandro Toledo) is in jail from 2023. (3) A further ex-president (Ollanta Humala) who was in a preventative prison was accused of corruption. And (4) a president (Pedro Pablo Kuczynski) was deposed for alleged acts of corruption.

should no longer be the "tail" but now are to be the "head of the nations." The explosive numerical growth in recent years is a clear "sign from God" that they should abandon their traditional apoliticism and now assume responsibility for governing the nations.

Second, conservative Protestants affirm that a born-again child of God is sufficiently qualified to be a competent political authority and a capable public servant (functionary). This explains their lack of interest in political training and their lack of experience in involvement in public administration, and their indifference toward the processes of mobilizing civil society.

Third, they believe they are divinely predestined "to morally redefine" the nation, and that they are the only ones who are qualified to legislate and govern according to God's will. They claim that "worldly" politicians do not have God's blessing to govern adequately. They either ignore or do not want to admit that politics has its own rules, such as agreements, compromises, the search for consensus, under-the-table agreements, and working with those whose interests might not be genuine or pure.

Fourth, they are convinced that the defense of the traditional family is a winning political issue that can mobilize the majority of Protestants. This becomes political capital that can catapult them into strategic positions of governing authority. They show little to no interest in social or political problems such as poverty (or extreme poverty), systemic corruption, violence against women, the exclusion of minorities, responsible care of our shared habitat, or constructing a society where everyone has equal value.

All these reasons explain why, having been reactionary toward democratic principles and believing in a theocratic model of government, they believe that the State and public functionaries must serve their religious vision of life and political interests. This also explains why they consider that public policies need to be based only on religious criteria and that religious believers are better citizens than unbelievers and are the best qualified to govern the nations.

The Current Protestant Incursion into Politics

The tense Church-State relationship, just like conflicts between the church and the surrounding society, is not a new phenomenon in the history of the Christian faith. Although we are not always aware of this, from their beginning in the first century, Christian communities had to interact, directly or indirectly, with those who exercised political power. "From its beginning, the Christian

Church confronted the necessity of locating itself in the political, cultural, and religious world that it had to direct its message to, be responsible for its presence in, and respond to its demands, questionings, and attacks."[8]

Nevertheless, it is necessary to highlight that the current incursion of Protestants into the field of politics began with greater visibility in the 1980s, with the formation of evangelical political parties in various countries in Latin America and the Caribbean. The process itself in fact began decades earlier. From the middle of the 1960s a process of contextual theological reflection-action had begun with the founding of the Latin America Theological Fellowship (Fraternidad Teológica Latinoamericana / FTL). FTL was – and continues to be – a space where Protestant pastors, theologians, biblical scholars, and social activists could gather. They began to articulate what later would become known as "integral mission."

Within this process of contextual theological reflection-action, the Lausanne Covenant (1974) and the Jarabacoa Declaration (1983) were key documents. They began articulating a vision of social and political action with Protestant roots. These documents stated that both the verbal proclamation of the gospel and social and political responsibility were legitimate dimensions of Christian witness in the world.[9]

There has been an abundant diversity of research regarding national experiences from the 1980s and the 1990s which analyzes the processes of the Protestant incursion into politics in Latin America. The studies describe both positive and negative aspects of this movement from an apolitical position

---

8. Míguez Bonino, *Poder del Evangelio*, 7.

9. Pedro Arana, ed., *Teología en el Camino: Documentos presentados en los últimos veinte años por diferentes comunidades cristianas de América Latina* (Lima: Presencia, 1983), 31–42, 125–41.

to a growing participation in public life: in Peru,[10] Argentina,[11] Guatemala,[12] Mexico,[13] and Chile.[14]

Paul Freston carried out important comparative and analytical research on Protestant political participation in Latin America. His work was aided by Protestant researchers with numerous case studies from Mexico, Guatemala, Nicaragua, Peru, and Brazil.[15] Freston also realized a much larger comparative and analytical study with case studies from Asia, Africa, and Latin America, selecting for the Latin American region experiences from Argentina, Mexico, Chile, Colombia, Peru, Nicaragua, and Guatemala.[16] It is also important to consider the research carried out, with a large comparative analysis, by academicians such as Virginia Garrard-Burnett and David Stoll.[17]

More recently, Luis Pérez Guadalupe and Sebastián Grundberger, with the collaboration of Catholic and Protestant scholars, edited a book that rigorously analyzed the political experiences of Protestants during the last two decades in Argentina, Brazil, Chile, Colombia, Costa Rica, El Salvador, Guatemala, Mexico, Panama, and Peru.[18]

---

10. Darío López, *Los Evangélicos y los Derechos Humanos: La experiencia social del Concilio Nacional Evangélico del Perú 1980-1992* (Lima: Centro Evangélico de Misiología Andino-Amazónica, 1998); Darío López, *La Seducción del Poder: Los evangélicos y la política en el Perú de los noventa* (Lima: Instituto de Ciencias Políticas, Investigación y Promoción del Desarrollo "Nueva Humanidad," 2004); José Luis Pérez Guadalupe, *Entre Dios y el César: El impacto político de los evangélicos en el Perú y en América Latina* (Lima: Instituto de Estudios Social Cristianos-Konrad Adenauer Stifung, 2017); Tomás Gutiérrez, "Protestantismo y Política en América Latina: una interpretación desde las Ideologías Políticas, Siglo XX" (PhD diss., Universidad Nacional Mayor de San Marcos, 2017).

11. Hilario Wynarczyk, *Ciudadanos de dos mundos: El movimiento evangélico en la vida pública argentina 1980-2001* (Buenos Aires: UNSAM EDITA de Universidad Nacional de General San Martín, 2009).

12. Virginia Garrard-Burnett, ed., *El protestantismo en Guatemala: Viviendo en la Nueva Jerusalén* (Guatemala: Piedra Santa, 2009).

13. Mariano Ávila, *Entre Dios y el César: Líderes evangélicos y política en México (1992-2002)* (Grand Rapids: Libros Desafío, 2008).

14. Evguenia Pediakova, *Evangélicos, política y sociedad en Chile: Dejando "el refugio de las masas" 1990-2010* (Huelpen: Centro Evangélico de Estudios Pentecostales-Instituto de Estudios Avanzados, Universidad de Santiago de Chile, 2013).

15. Paul Freston, ed., *Evangelical Christianity and Democracy in Latin America* (Oxford: Oxford University Press, 2008).

16. Paul Freston, *Evangelicals and Politics in Asia, Africa, and Latin America* (Cambridge: Cambridge University Press, 2001).

17. Virginia Garrard-Burnett and David Stoll, eds., *Rethinking Protestantism in Latin America* (Philadelphia: Temple University Press, 1993); Virginia Garrard-Burnett, ed., *On Earth as It Is in Heaven: Religion in Modern Latin America* (Wilmington: Scholarly Resources, 2000).

18. Pérez Guadalupe and Grundberger, *Evangélicos y poder*.

Toward the end of the 1990s, the presence of Protestants in the political arena was summarized like this: "This participation is not sustained in the relatively neutral environment of education and service. It has erupted directly in the life of party politics, whether through involvement in political parties, by forming their particular 'currents' within existing parties, or by attempting to create 'evangelical' parties."[19]

Regarding this topic, Pérez Guadalupe and Grundberger critically analyzed the political experience of evangelicals in recent years. They stated that this process had three stages or moments, which they named "the three historical models of evangelical political participation":

> *(1) The Evangelical Political Party:* is the confessional movement or party consisting of and led exclusively by "evangelical brothers and sisters," who under a "religious mandate" desire to obtain control of the government in their nations so that, from that point, they will be able to evangelize more effectively. . . . Their political objectives are merely instrumental and strategic, given that their real intention is to obtain the power to govern religiously – some would say theocratically – and to evangelize. The intention to form confessional movements or parties has taken place in almost all of the countries in the region since the decade of the 1980s. In every case they have failed. They have not achieved unified support from their brothers and sisters in the faith, and even less from non-evangelical voters. . . . *(2) The Evangelical Front:* refers to a political "front" led by evangelical Christians from different denominations, but which is open to other people who identify with the political ideals (although not fully with their religious ideals); in these cases, they, in effect, reduce their religious principles in order to maximize, pragmatically, their political possibilities. . . . *(3) The Evangelical Faction:* consists of the participation of evangelical leaders in electoral processes within already established political parties or movements, based on electoral alliances (but without having the ability to lead such a movement or party). . . . This is the model that has produced the best results up until now.[20]

This is an accurate description. The model that has yielded the best results during recent years has been what Pérez Guadalupe and Grundberger call "the

---

19. Miguez Bonino, *Poder del Evangelio*, 11–12.
20. Pérez Guadalupe and Grundberger, *Evangélicos y poder*, 53–55.

evangelical faction."²¹ It is interesting to note that, in more than one case in the region's countries, it was the church leaders who negotiated the quota of listed candidates, in exchange for assuring the political parties or movements of the homogeneous and guaranteed votes of their church members. The authors write that "some evangelical leaders want to extend their religious activity into political spheres and convert the 'religious capital' they have acquired into valuable 'political capital.'"²²

The presence of the nondemocratic sector of evangelical churches in the public arena, in alliance with charismatic and neo-Pentecostal churches, is not a novelty in Spanish-speaking Latin America and the Caribbean. As has already been mentioned, there have been positive and negative examples. There have been lamentable experiences, such as the public support by evangelical pastors of the Augusto Pinochet dictatorship in Chile (1973–1990), the total defense of the dictatorial regime of Alberto Fujimori (1990–2000) by sectors of the Peruvian evangelical community, as well as the support given in Guatemala to dictators Efraín Ríos Montt, accused of genocide (1982–1983), and Jorge Antonio Serrano Elías, charged with corruption (1991–1993). Given their positive legacy of a healthy exercise of power, we have quite different examples in the Brazilians Benedita da Silva (congressional representative and senator, and governor of the State of Rio de Janeiro) and Marina Silva (congressional representative and senator, minister of the environment, and candidate for the presidency).

Regarding the current incursion into politics by nondemocratic evangelicals, the recent history of Brazil provides an account of their political-electoral face and of how their presence in the public arena can be interpreted:

> The Pentecostal churches have been a key factor in taking this fascist-tinted discourse (misogynous, homophobic, and racist) to the poorest sectors. In the last stretch of his campaign, Bolsonaro obtained the support of the powerful Iglesia Universal del Reino de Dios [Universal Church of the Kingdom of God], also known

---

21. Recent experience in the last two decades in Peru confirms this analysis. Evangelicals – pastors and lay leaders – who reached Peru's Congress were elected as candidates of nonconfessional political parties or movements: during the government of Alejandro Toledo 2001–2006 (Walter Alejos, Perú Posible); Alan García 2006–2011 (Aida Lazo, Restauración Nacional; Maria Sumiri, Partido Nacionalista); Ollanta Humala 2011–2016 (Eduardo Nayap, Partido Nacionalista; Julio Rosas, Fujimorian; Humberto Lay, Alianza por el Gran Cambio); and Pedro Pablo Kuczynski 2016–2018 (Juan Carlos González and Tamar Arinburgo, Fujimorians; Moisés Gula Piantos, Peruanos por el Kambio; Julio Rosas, Alianza para el Progreso, and later nonpartisan).

22. Pérez Guadalupe and Grundberger, *Evangélicos y poder*, 12.

by the name of its television program, "Pare de sufrir" [Stop Suffering].[23]

Regarding the relationship between neo-Pentecostals and Bolsonaro, it is stated, "The recent history of Brazil demonstrates that the parliamentary coup and the growing political importance of an anticommunist evangelicalism have resulted in creating this person who not only represents antidemocracy and antiprogressivism but has explicitly promised to end this [Communist] current."[24]

Two questions arise: Do all evangelicals have the same understanding of politics and political action, the same political/electoral preferences or sympathy, the same partisan commitment? Is there a political homogeneity within the Latin American and Caribbean evangelical community? The answer to both questions is "no." Within evangelical churches, there are different political positions and a plurality of partisan political postures.[25]

The various political positions that evangelicals have held and continue to hold in diverse contexts and realities demonstrate that they have not always been apolitical and opposed to politics, believers in political abstentionism, defenders of the status quo, those who justify repressive regimes, or enthusiastic promoters of a "social strike." In fact, those evangelicals who claimed to be apolitical and against getting involved in politics always were and still are anti-communist, anti-ecumenical, and defenders of Zionism. In other words, they were not apolitical. Behind their apparent retreat from the world and their indifference to politics was a political posture that could not be covered up and which, more than once, led them to support, legitimize, and justify dictatorial regimes that violated human rights or "democracies" in which the large majority of citizens were treated as human refuse.

Living in a Democracy

Considering that it is not easy to predict future political actions in the variety of historical contexts in which they happen, it is important to keep the following key concepts in mind in order to anticipate possible scenarios:

---

23. Oscar Miranda, "Jair Bolsonaro: La amenaza fascista," *La República*, 14 October 2018, 11.

24. Alberto Adrianzén, "Brasil y el futuro de América del Sur," *La República*, 17 October 2018, 11.

25. Freston, *Evangelical Christianity and Democracy in Latin America*, 3, 5.

1. The changing social and political processes in each nation within the region.
2. The continuing fragmentation of the evangelical community.
3. The evangelical community's connection or nonconnection with organized civil society.
4. The emergence of messianic and authoritarian leaders.
5. These leaders' relationships with traditional politicians or with new political movements.

Nevertheless, considering the political experiences of recent years, one issue is abundantly clear: evangelicals do not have identical sympathies, interests, orientations, or political commitments. In other words, rather than uniformity, there is a heterogeneity of sympathies, interests, orientations, and political commitments that appears during electoral processes or political debates about public issues.

In addition, it is important to consider the attention and interest evangelicals with little experience in democracy give to current polemical, controversial, and debatable topics on the public agenda, particularly their opposition to the rights of sexual minorities (the LGBTI+ community) and to abortion in all its forms, as well as their closed-minded defense of the traditional family and their opposition to the focus on gender in education and public health. It becomes clear that their immediate objective is to intervene in governmental policies so that they are shaped by and respond to their political-religious interests.

What is paradoxical is that, although evangelicals with little experience in democracy do not want the State to impose sensible public policies upon them, for example in the areas of sex education or orientation, they do desire public policies that have a religious stamp. In other words, they do not want the State to impose public policies that go against their faith or against the "natural order" or the "original design for the family," but they do want public policies to be constructed according to their religious beliefs. This is made clear in Peru by the opinion of the visible spokesperson of the program Con mis hijos no te metas (Don't mess with my children). The real interest of the undemocratic evangelicals is made clear:

> We conservatives desire that the State not claim authority to make our private and intimate decisions; that politicians (and public policies) do not intervene in our feelings, thoughts, or beliefs. We seek that the State respect our inherent freedom and the established order, and that they stop imposing their

particular, ideological vision on citizens as if we were subjects of an authoritarian government that was delirious with claiming to be sovereign.[26]

It can therefore be concluded that, for this sector of the evangelical community, to live in a democracy is difficult. In a democracy it is expected that dialogue, tolerance, and respect are preferred over monologue, intolerance, and disrespect for those who think and live differently than the established conventions and the religious beliefs of the majority or minorities of the population. For those nondemocratic evangelicals, dialogue is perceived as a betrayal of one's faith, tolerance is a sign of weakness and surrender, and respect for a neighbor who thinks and lives differently is seen as an abdication of one's missionary and evangelizing vocation. Their political-social option will always be a theocracy in which all live according to their exclusive religious principles.

Keeping in mind the way the nondemocratic evangelicals understand democracy, politics, and citizenship, it is important to affirm that politics is not limited, nor needs to be limited, to political parties or occasional elections. Politics is also connected to the actions of organized civil society, of social movements, and with the creation of social capital that contributes to democracy.

Perhaps this is the best collective path or road that religious sectors like nondemocratic evangelicals – in reality all evangelicals – need to travel or follow, in order to better understand what it means and implies to be democratic and live in a democracy. In particular, learning how to live day by day in dialogue, tolerance, respect, and peace is better practice and citizenship conduct than monologue, intolerance, disrespect, and verbal or physical violence.

One fact of the current context should serve as a warning not to be naïve in this field. Currently in Latin America, not only is politics for sale, but, sadly, so is religion. Politicians and religious leaders use churches for electoral purposes, to justify and legitimize repressive acts against citizens, and as an instrument of social control of the population. They use the Bible as a type of magic charm to justify their addiction to power, and prayer to legitimize the violation of human rights. In addition, professional politicians know that they have to follow certain steps if they want to obtain the support of the undemocratic evangelicals who are interested in getting involved in public policies with the goal of imposing their religious vision of life upon all citizens.

---

26. Christian Rosas, Facebook, 15 August 2019, 11:03 a.m.

Seasoned politicians know that the following steps are necessary to obtain the trust and support of nondemocratic evangelicals: (1) Establish a relationship with the pastor of an urban "megachurch" that is economically powerful, who has a significant presence throughout social media, and who has a number of members as a voting bloc; (2) attend worship services and give the impression that you are a "born-again" Christian; (3) let the pastor "lay hands" on you, anoint you, and publicly pray for you; (4) identify publicly with the topics that are most important for the majority of evangelicals (the defense of the traditional family, opposition to all forms of abortion, among others), in essence giving the impression that you are an active defender of the political-religious interests of the pro-life and pro-family groups; (5) present yourself as a mediator between the State and the minority churches. It is even better if someone "prophesies" over such politicians or has had a vision in which they are seen as having won the presidency or the congressional positions they are seeking. They also know that the evangelicals represent important political capital and an electoral "bloc" that should not be underestimated. Nevertheless, the social and political aspirations of evangelicals (full religious liberty, equality of opportunities, the separation of the Catholic Church from the State) are not important for most of these politicians, just their votes to help them get elected.

They also take advantage of the political inexperience of the majority of evangelical pastors who, in recent years, have sought to get close to political authorities with three basic goals in mind: (1) To pray for these politicians; (2) to give them a Bible as a present; and (3) to have a picture taken of them with these officials. The majority of these pastors do not have the political background or training, the firsthand knowledge of the national reality, the experience in civic-initiated projects, direct relationships with organized civic society, nor the ethical foundations of moving in circles other than religious spheres. In other words, their lack of experience in political matters makes them easy prey for professional politicians who are accustomed to manipulating, misleading, lying to, and utilizing social sectors that are not well informed on political issues.

Do evangelicals, just like other people in the full exercise of their citizenship rights, have an interest in knowing about and participating actively in politics? Yes. The double citizenship that they have (as citizens of the kingdom of God and as citizens of the *polis*) implies, among other things, that it is their right and their responsibility to seek the peace of the city where they live. They are to commit themselves to every action that contributes to the common good and to the justice and full respect of human life and dignity. But this means a personal vocation and commitment that can be expressed through political parties and social movements. It does not mean an institutional or organizational option that compromises a church, denomination, or religious institution. The reason for this is clear: within churches, there exist many diverse political leanings, preferences, options, commitments, and opinions. Out of respect for this diversity, institutionally, churches should never align themselves completely with a specific political party. Church members, in the exercise of their citizenship, individually have this right and, following their consciences, can get involved with and support the political party of their choice.

The problem is not resolved, however, by affirming that the participation of religious believers in political life is as equally valid as any other commitment in society. Nor is it resolved by affirming that politics is a legitimate mission field for believers. Information from recent decades indicates that when evangelicals get involved in politics without adequate experience, knowledge, and the skill that is required for a field that has its own rules, it is easy for them to fall into the same vices as professional politicians (nepotism, corruption, crooked deals made under the table, the purchase of votes, among others). In other words, good intentions and a good personal testimony are not enough, especially when we travel in a world that requires solid ethics, a firsthand knowledge, and ability to legislate through parliaments or government institutions. Politics is not for the naïve or unprepared. It is for those who have the vocation and who are prepared to navigate the field of politics. And, of course, not all evangelicals (nor all citizens) have the vocation to become politicians.

Finally, regarding politics, all citizens, whether religiously active or not, need to understand that full citizenship and involvement in public life needs to be expressed in concrete actions. These actions should contribute toward the construction of democracy where citizens have equality of opportunity, the search for the common good, and justice. These are more important than campaign promises that are never fulfilled or laws that are never implemented. In this sense, everybody needs to exercise civic watchfulness. This means that we demand from politicians and government officials transparency regarding their actions, financial transparency, good use of taxpayers' money, and open access to information. This responsible citizenship action requires evangelicals to understand and be prepared to debate issues in the public arena with politicians or civic society leaders. This means having firsthand knowledge and training in politics, plus an ability to enter into dialogue, tolerance, and respect for opinions that are different from our own. This is important because religious language does not communicate well in the public sphere, not because it is not valid, but because it is not understandable for those who do not move in religious circles. The task before us is to articulate in a language that is comprehensible to those in the public arena the convictions of our Christian faith and identity.

References

Adrianzén, Alberto. "Brasil y el futuro de América del Sur." *La República*, 17 October 2018.

Arana, Pedro, ed. *Teología en el Camino: Documentos presentados en los últimos veinte años por diferentes comunidades cristianas de América Latina*. Lima: Presencia, 1983.

Ávila, Mariano. *Entre Dios y el César: Líderes evangélicos y política en México (1992–2002)*. Grand Rapids: Libros Desafío, 2008.

Fonseca, Juan. *Misioneros y Civilizadores: Protestantismo y modernización en el Perú (1915–1930)*. Lima: Fondo Editorial de la Pontificia Universidad Católica del Perú, 2002.

Freston, Paul, ed. *Evangelical Christianity and Democracy in Latin America*. Oxford: Oxford University Press, 2008.

———. *Evangelicals and Politics in Asia, Africa, and Latin America*. Cambridge: Cambridge University Press, 2001.

Garrard-Burnett, Virginia, ed. *On Earth as It Is in Heaven: Religion in Modern Latin America*. Wilmington: Scholarly Resources, 2000.

———, ed. *El protestantismo en Guatemala: Viviendo en la Nueva Jerusalén*. Guatemala: Piedra Santa, 2009.

Garrard-Burnett, Virginia, and David Stoll, eds. *Rethinking Protestantism in Latin America*. Philadelphia: Temple University Press, 1993.

Gutiérrez, Tomás. "Protestantismo y Política en América Latina: una interpretación desde las Ideologías Políticas, Siglo XX." PhD diss., Universidad Nacional Mayor de San Marcos, 2017.

López, Darío. *Los Evangélicos y los Derechos Humanos: La experiencia social del Concilio Nacional Evangélico del Perú 1980–1992*. Lima: Centro Evangélico de Misiología Andino-Amazónica, 1998.

———. "Protestantismo y espiritualidad en América Latina." In *¿Hacia dónde va el Protestantismo en América Latina?*, edited by H. Fernando Bullón and Nicolás Panotto, 159–71. Buenos Aires: Kairós, 2017.

———. *La Seducción del Poder: Los evangélicos y la política en el Perú de los noventa*. Lima: Instituto de Ciencias Políticas, Investigación y Promoción del Desarrollo "Nueva Humanidad," 2004.

Míguez Bonino, José. *Poder del evangelio y poder político: La participación de los evangélicos en la política de América Latina*. Buenos Aires: Kairós, 1999.

Miranda, Oscar. "Jair Bolsonaro: La amenaza fascista." *La República*, 14 October 2018.

Mondragón, Carlos. *Leudar la masa: El pensamiento social de los protestantes en América Latina: 1920–1950*. Buenos Aires: Kairós, 2005.

Padilla, C. René. *Discipulado y misión: Compromiso con el Reino de Dios*. Buenos Aires: Kairós, 1997.

———. "Los evangélicos: Nuevos actores en el escenario político latinoamericano." In *De la marginación al compromiso: Los evangélicos y la política en América Latina*, edited by C. René Padilla, 5–19. Buenos Aires: Fraternidad Teológica Latinoamericana, 1991.

Pediakova, Evguenia. *Evangélicos, política y sociedad en Chile: Dejando "el refugio de las masas" 1990–2010*. Huelpen: Centro Evangélico de Estudios Pentecostales-Instituto de Estudios Avanzados, Universidad de Santiago de Chile, 2013.

Pérez Guadalupe, José Luis. *Entre Dios y el César: El impacto político de los evangélicos en el Perú y en América Latina*. Lima: Instituto de Estudios Social Cristianos-Konrad Adenauer Stifung, 2017.

Pérez Guadalupe, José Luis, and Sebastián Grundberger, eds. *Evangélicos y poder en América Latina*. Lima: Instituto de Estudios Social Cristianos-Konrad Adenauer Stifung, 2018.

Wynarczyk, Hilario. *Ciudadanos de dos mundos: El movimiento evangélico en la vida pública argentina 1980–2001*. Buenos Aires: UNSAM EDITA de Universidad Nacional de General San Martín, 2009.

9

Decolonizing Christianity
Clothing Ourselves in the Gospel of the Kingdom of God

Marcelo Vargas

To decolonize Christianity is to create in us a radical change in how we see and interpret the world: to feel it as it is, and consequently, to live in it in its fullness. How we perceive and feel the world that surrounds us, our worldview, is fundamental to our thinking and actions. It keeps us from being naïve and it helps us read our context with greater precision. This chapter is an approach in three areas: history, ecosystem, and theology, but without separating them. We need to recognize that each area overlaps the other two, which interact with and respect each other. History, ecosystem, and theology are disciplines that necessarily include one another, and that together cannot totally cover the theme at hand: decolonizing Christianity.

History

It was a cold winter morning. Túpac was crying, with his gaze lost in the Andean mountains of the Bolivian high plateau.

He was crying because fear had entered him and had deceived him for a long time. This will not be a tale, but rather an essay. Therefore, I will tell you straightaway why this Aymara was crying. It is not a pleasant topic . . . not by a long shot.

Túpac was crying on that dry, winter's day under an intense, cloudless blue-sky ceiling where the sun was shining brightly. He was crying because he had systematically and naïvely believed in shamelessly invented, false historical narratives.

Another Aymaran was walking nearby with his little llama. "Why are you crying?" he asked. Túpac answered, "I remember how our ancestors heard a voice that completely and radically transformed how we should understand life." Both men courageously raised their gaze to the horizon, eager to find out more.

What history have they been trying to tell us? How and when will we wake up?

This history which has been told us for centuries is an apocryphal, made-up version. It is similar to versions that today's dominant social media tell us about events that are happening. It is a false, distorted history with bad intentions that our internalized colonialism has promoted since the fifteenth century. It is a history that has been elaborated systematically and strategically by representatives of the status quo. It has been constructed by descendants of the Spanish who were perpetrators and accomplices of the arbitrary acts of evil committed against indigenous people and against the land that nourished them. They have persistently been telling everyone this "tall tale" with cruelty. As a result, confusion has spread against the backdrop of ignorance and abuse.

The continent of *Abya Yala*, land that is mature, land that is alive and flourishes, was so named by the Guna (indigenous people) in a language better suited and more appropriate than the Spanish language brought by the Spaniards. *Abya Yala* was inhabited by close to one hundred million Indians. Indians? What name is this? This name was imposed and continues to be a mistake because it belonged to people of another nation (India) located on the other side of the planet. The Europeans who imposed this name on the inhabitants of *Abya Yala* at the end of the fifteenth century announced, as they took possession of this territory by force, that they had "discovered" it, when in reality this continent had been inhabited for thousands of years and the people had maintained contact with Asia and with the Vikings.

The arrival of the Europeans in *Abya Yala* was a violent, bloody, genocidal invasion that enslaved the inhabitants. It was a military occupation in the fifteenth century with the modern weapons of its time and horrific techniques of mass destruction. The Europeans were insatiable mercenaries and a large percentage of them were delinquents who had been let out of Spanish and Portuguese jails. They were prisoners condemned for serious crimes who arrived in fleets of ships on a different continent. They were greedy men who, when they heard that there was much gold and silver, hurriedly came to make easy money, large fortunes, and then to return to Europe.

The utilitarian meaning that these men gave to their time in *Abya Yala* had the result that men from Castille, Extremadura, and Andalusia plundered the lands harshly with their swords, while the Basques dedicated themselves almost exclusively to the extraction of silver from the rich mountain of Potosi. They legalized the forced labor of the Andean indigenous people who were enslaved by the Spanish soldiers who turned them over in chains to work them to death.

With the immense silver deposits of the *Sumaj Orku* ("rich mountain" in Quechua), accidentally dug up by the indigenous Hualipa in 1542 in Potosi, Bolivia, a silver bridge could have been constructed from the mountain of Potosi all the way to Spain. The flow of silver from Potosi, the largest silver deposit in human history (containing 80 percent of the silver on the planet), activated the European economy to such a degree that this underdeveloped economy became the strongest economic system in the world. The new geopolitical center was no longer the Mediterranean, but rather the coasts of the Atlantic Ocean.

For centuries until the fifteenth century, the Arabs had dominated the world economic system. The Arabs and the Chinese were the cultures that created technology, science, and knowledge until the natural resources of *Abya Yala* began Modernity.[1] What made this change in the center of geopolitics possible? 5,450,000,000,000 pesos of silver were stolen from the Potosi mine, without counting what was extracted from the mine at Zapoteca, Mexico; without adding the silver that left the country as contraband or sank to the bottom of the sea; without counting the six million Aymaras and Quechuas enslaved in the mines. In 1573, barely thirty years after the founding of Potosi in Andean lands, the city already had 125,000 inhabitants, more than the population of cities such as Madrid, Seville, Rome, or Paris. In 1650 it had 160,000 inhabitants, which made it one of the largest cities in the world.[2]

When Christopher Columbus reached these lands, there were tens of millions of indigenous people who had inhabited the lands for thousands of years. Nevertheless, this Italian navigator from Genoa and his fleet financed

---

1. Enrique Dussel, "Europa, Modernidad y Eurocentrismo," in *La colonialidad del saber: eurocentrismo y ciencias sociales – Perspectivas Latinoamericanas*, ed. Edgardo Lander (Buenos Aires: CLACSO, 2000).

2. Eduardo Galeano, *Las venas abiertas de América Latina* (Buenos Aires: Siglo Veintiuno, 2004), 10–14.

by the king and queen of Spain thought that, upon reaching the shores of Guanabana (one of the Bahaman islands devastated in 2019 by Hurricane Dorian), he had reached India through a new route, thereby shortening the trip by sea to the Asian continent. This led him to believe that he was an expert navigator, and he was received as a hero in Spain. What he discovered, however, was not a new route to India, but something much more transcendental: *Abya Yala*. In addition, without realizing what he had done, he had become the first European to prove that the earth was round, although the Chinese had demonstrated this eight centuries earlier.

From the moment the Europeans, who felt themselves to be missionaries of the papacy, landed in indigenous land, they were accompanied by official Roman Catholic religious representatives in order to provide legality and credibility to their acts of genocide. The priests and bishops (with some notable exceptions) gave their blessing to the atrocities that were committed. In other words, the cross, the Bible, and the Roman Catholic religion gave their stamp of approval to the violence. As many scholars have pointed out, the indigenous population of Peru and Upper Peru (Bolivia) was reduced from 8 million inhabitants to 1.3 million between 1530 and 1580.[3]

The Spanish and Portuguese invasion, and later the English invasion further north, did not achieve its objective of eliminating the indigenous presence on the continent. The most numerous groups (Aymara, Quechua, and Guarani) strengthened their identity. The abuses and atrocities committed by the Europeans led to a passive, secretive resistance generally, and, in some instances, organized violent resistance. The conflict of cultures imposed by the foreigners resulted in a period of mutual interaction that forced the indigenous people to adapt and change their worldviews, although these adaptations were constantly resisted.

The European mission was to replace the worldviews and spirituality of the indigenous inhabitants, but it was not accomplished. Both soldiers and priests brought a message that was strongly Eurocentric and radically opposed to the affirmation, recognition, and acceptance of the full humanity of the original people groups.

At the beginning of the European invasion, this history was covered up . . . but not completely. It was a false story without ethical constraints, but it was filled with speculation and evil. Later, in the independent Latin American

---

3. Bartolomé Arzans de Orsúa y Vela, *El mundo desde Potosí: Vida y reflexiones de Bartolomé Arzans de Orsúa y Vela (1676–1736) – Selección, prólogo y notas de Mariano Baptista Gumucio* (Santa Cruz: Grupo Santander Central Hispano, 2000).

republics which were ruled by descendants of the Spanish and Portuguese, something similar happened. It was the continuation of a historical narrative that was an accomplice of the massacre of the people of *Abya Yala*. The same thing happens today. The owners of mass media and social networks continue to distort the truth. The news that is emphasized comes previously and horribly selected without regard for the veracity of the events (with rare exceptions). The history that "sells" is dominated by communication that is already accepted. There is nothing new under the sun. The history that was distorted before continues to be distorted right up to our times.

The fatuous use of information in the telling of the events that are concentrated in some individuals who are "experts" in historiography has distorted the correct understanding of the course of human history. Evangelical (or Protestant) historians, as they narrate their own stories, are not free from a slanted bias which has adjusted to the dominant academic assumptions. Comprehension of the events has been "inoculated" by the experts of reality. The understanding of the events by the overwhelming majority of the participants (the indigenous people) is almost never taken into consideration.

The historical legacy of European Protestant identity and spirituality in the nineteenth century was transferred to and developed by churches in the United States of America. The twenty-first century needs an "unmasking" of its categories and an analysis in light of the Bible, from the context of Latin America, faced with the gospel of the kingdom of God incarnated and proclaimed by Jesus Christ.

In this chapter, we seek consciously and intentionally the dismantling of the deceitful categories that continue in the historical, ecological, and theological fields. Two concepts of life entered into conflict in *Abya Yala*. One considered the indigenous person to be devoid of the ability to reason, but sufficiently good to serve those who considered themselves endowed with that ability (Juan Ginés de Sepúlveda, Spanish Catholic priest, 1494–1573). The invaders were possessed by a hallucination that caused them to have gold and silver fever. The other way to conceive life was the *Abya Yala* way, which was relational, communitarian, and united holistically with the cosmos.

The indigenous people were not greedy for the use of money, nor did they have the desire to increase their capital, nor the practice of private property. The gold and silver they collected from the rivers and rocks were used to create beautiful works of art to adorn their temples. What they expected from life was to survive by satisfying the needs of their community without damaging their unique and diverse ecological environment, by humbly taking care of and respecting Mother Earth.

Nevertheless, is this anarchy that has happened throughout history merely human? Is this what we believe? Or does there exist another space for powerful beings? There are spaces filled with evil spirits, where the conflict is even more intense. Not one drop of human blood falls to the ground except for the evil being who commands infernal troops, who lies without scruple, who aspires to control the world, who disseminates false history, who spreads the temptation to destroy one's neighbor and creation. Nevertheless, One with human blood overturns the evil being's pretentions, fury, and usurpations. When the Lamb/Lion is manifested again and returns in human flesh, the evil times will be gone forever. Evil will be eradicated when he appears. In the meantime, while events run their course, the enemy intruder will try to make a lifegiving encounter with the Lamb/Lion, both in community and personally, impossible.

What motivates our conscience? How have we conducted our lives, both in the world and in the church? Are we the keepers of the collective memory? Is our reading of history done with integrity, truth, and sincerity? Are we like survival machines, blindly programmed automatons? Has our conduct adjusted according to human wisdom, but not according to God's wisdom and grace? As 2 Corinthians 1:12 states: "Now this is our boast: Our conscience testifies that we have conducted ourselves in the world, and especially in our relations with you, with integrity and godly sincerity. We have done so, relying not on worldly wisdom but on God's grace."

When people who follow Christ in Latin America submerge themselves in the teaching of the apostle Paul, they do not easily adjust to the traditional history of "human wisdom" but rather to the truth. They interpret and experience history in a different way. They make a new reading of how we have come to this place. Freed from the hypocritical Eurocentrism, they listen with interest to the indigenous history. They say goodbye to false desires and fears, in order to give honor and loyalty to the Lord of history.

It is necessary to "reread" everything with new eyes – history and society, which is most relevant and liberating. To dissent with violent rebellion, to condemn with an inhuman rage, to desire vengeance, or to fill one's heart with resentment would be a domesticating stupidity. An alternative is to dissent by constructing a new reading of the previous historical context, including the history of Christianity, courageously changing old ways of thinking, by incorporating convictions that decolonize, unmask, and tear down current assumptions that cover up human guilt. This is a "rereading" that we need.

Ecosystem

"Please tell me now what happened to our ancestors, what they would say about history. I want to hear them," said the friend. "What did they do to the earth that nourished them as a mother? How did they treat the earth?"

"Ah," said Túpac. "That is a very, very bad thing. It is depressing," he said, shaking his head.

"Please, please," said the *Abya Yala* Aymara friend, "don't just sit there staring. In this pitcher there is a drink made from quinoa that grows in the high Andean mountains."

Both the indigenous people of *Abya Yala* and the African slaves who were brought to Brazil by the Portuguese, or those exploited by the Spanish in their colonies, and later by the Anglo-Saxons in the North or in the Caribbean, had a greatly appreciated culture and conservation of their habitat. They maintained a relationship of mutual dependence, of care and respect for their natural environment. The African slaves and the indigenous people of *Abya Yala* took care of nature by committing themselves to it. The oral history that they received from their ancestors had prepared them for it. The worldview that they had, especially their foundational beliefs, guided their behavior.

An example that persists up to today is the belief in the Pachamama, an essential deity of the Andean worldview. The Pachamama is perceived by her followers as demanding, furious, and punishing, but she is also seen as a generous and faithful provider. She is feared and must be pleased, satisfied, and made happy, because if she is not, she reacts and pays out retribution to the same degree. She sends out rays that burn, destructive winds, torrential rains, and frost and snow that kill crops and harvests. There is a constant relationship of magical fear, but this oppressive relationship is balanced by a component of respectful acknowledgment for her provision of everything that sustains life. The belief that tolerates the hard line of the Pachamama, but at the same time values her generosity, provides space for the *ayni*, the loyal retribution of the indigenous believer. The beneficiaries of her administration, although they have also suffered her punishment, offer reverence to the Pachamama for both the bad and the good that she has sent. The indigenous worldview is not dualistic. It does not contrast good and evil in conflict. It allows both to coexist in harmony. Its logic includes at least a third element, perhaps more.

Which communities on earth are without a doubt guardians of the ecosystem? What is the worldview that functions in the people who have a relationship of mutuality with nature? In order to obtain the appreciation for the creation that indigenous people have, they have developed a logic that is not a dualistic bivalent. The most deeply rooted logic in Western culture is dualistic, which, in addition to being superficial, puts elements into exclusive conflict without being open to a middle ground: good and evil, black and white, body and soul, faith and works, human beings and nature, body and spirit. In contrast, trivalent or polyvalent indigenous logic provides opportunity for at least a third option. It is inclusive and does not seek conflict. It is a different way to look at life, a way that builds holistic, harmonious relationships with the cosmos.

Our planet faces an enormous and irreversible problem in the twenty-first century. The problem goes beyond every religion, culture, political party, or hegemonic country. It affects everyone. All of us will need to join together for one simple reason. Our concern must not be temporary, local, or isolated. It must be holistic.

If we stopped driving our cars today on a global level, or if all agricultural industry were stopped today, with the information that scientists have they predict that the current global warming of 1.2 to 1.7 degrees Celsius would reach a 3 degrees Celsius warming by the end of the century. If we do not stop the level of current activity it will rise between 4 and 5 degrees.[4]

Previously there have been, at various times, great extinctions of living species. Sixty-five million years ago, dinosaurs disappeared; 95 percent of the then living species died out with only a two-degree increase in the global temperature.[5] This sixth extinction that is currently occurring is the first that is primarily due to the activity of humanity. The previous five extinctions were a consequence of large natural phenomena. The questions that we need to ask are: What will life look like after this global warming? Who will survive? It will not be this generation that will suffer the consequences of their irresponsibility. We are technologically advanced but have no moral will to take care of our common habitat. It will be the third or fourth generation that will experience the devastating results.

How do we respond to the greatest environmental threat in the history of humanity? The current crisis is unprecedented. A lethal infection is now

---

4. A. Vilches et al., "Frenar el cambio climático," online article, 2014, accessed 10 September 2020, https://www.researchgate.net/publication/302295798_Frenar_el_Cambio_Climatico.

5. BioLogos, "Why Should Christians Care for Creation?," 7 December 2019, accessed 10 September 2020, https://biologos.org/common-questions/why-should-christians-care-for-creation.

affecting our planet. It is so sick that biodiversity scientists themselves think that we have gone past the point of no return. We are beyond the limit at which our planetary organism could recover its health naturally.[6] Faced with this reflection, "let's roll up our sleeves and get to work."

Independently of the concepts that we have about God and what is sacred, everything ends here. There is no escape from this planet. We therefore have the responsibility to develop a common humanitarian and planetary conscience. We live on a poisoned planet. We have land, air, and water pollution. One in every four persons dies prematurely due to air pollution, mainly in cities. Unknown diseases in birds, animals, plants, insects, and fish all lead to the same conclusion: the damage from agricultural toxins and plastics is an environmental crime.

The other sphere of power has led Mother Earth to moan in pain for a long time. Nevertheless, the devastating death has allowed something different to come in, something so big, so joyful, and so real that the inhuman troops have been left unable to move. The human Lamb/Lion is actively on the move, weakening the charm of the accuser, the destroyer, the prince who is the supreme liar in narrating human history.

To dissent by substituting beliefs about history incites people to attempt to restore the ecosystem motivated by love, an essential component of human life. It is necessary to take acts of resistance against capitalism, against transnational companies, against consumerism, against (greedy) individualism. Without a doubt, these daring activities should be motivated by love for the Creator of those who strive, first and foremost, for zero growth, to be followed by a decrease in the economies, among other actions. For example, Bolivia, the poorest country in South America, cannot provide employment and food for the majority of its people, who are poor, because just a few families, rich families who would all fit in one room, own more than 50 percent of the country's land and wealth.[7] The wealth generated by the country should be distributed more fairly among everyone.

---

6. A. Vilches et al., "Biodiversidad," 2014, accessed 3 September 2020, https://www.researchgate.net/publication/302790840_Biodiversidad.

7. Comisión Episcopal de Pastoral Social Cáritas Bolivia, "Ricos y pobres: la brecha se ensancha," *Revista de Análisis Económico* vol. 19 (2004).

Theology

> "Friend," said Túpac, "when a man begins an adventure like this one, he should say goodbye to false hopes and false fears, because otherwise death or freedom will arrive too late to save honor and Mother Earth.
>
> "In addition, the Lord and King, the Lamb/Lion, is actively on the move."
>
> A strange feeling came upon them. The Kingdom of kingdoms was preparing for its full arrival. The trees seemed to be moving as if they were dancing, and the animals were living in harmony.

Contemporary Christianity has resulted in the expansion of the Western epistemological, religious, economic, and political system. This system is characterized not by a holistic, inclusive vision, but rather by the rationalist postulates of the Greek philosophers and by the coalition of the Renaissance and the Enlightenment. This Christianity has blocked the world from hearing and receiving the gospel of the kingdom of God. It has diluted, divided, and distorted the full integrity of the message that Jesus Christ proclaimed, taught, and lived.

The fatuous use of reason, by concentrating on the production of ideas in some enlightened individuals, causes sin in various ways: it has falsified history; it has distorted the Creator and Lord; it has magnified a different Christ; it has continuously dehumanized our planet's inhabitants. But this is not all. It has continued to conspire against the ecological equilibrium of nature by destroying it beyond repair. From a new vision of history, located outside the system of domination, we can bring about an authentic restoration of spirituality. This can shape an individual and community identity, but with a decolonizing perspective of evangelical faith.

Is this decolonization possible from within evangelical Christianity, given that it is the result of a coalition between modernity and colonialism? In order to transform this dominant ideology, we need to weave a perspective from an indigenous worldview. We can expect that this new vision would not have a dualistic logic, but one that would be holistic, inclusive, and multidimensional, and that would appreciate Jesus Christ in a new way. This (new?) reading makes it possible to create a new space that brings together truth and freedom.

It should be noted that Jesus and Paul rejected the intellectualism of the religious Jews. They situated themselves against the dead letter, against the dichotomy of Greek philosophy. The Jewish leaders who had an endless list of rules corroborated by their thought and practice that they had distanced themselves from the spirit of the Scriptures and from a personal relationship with God.

The theology of holistic mission was born immersed in the postulates and rules of Western theology. It was born as an academicist theology. From its beginning, it has adopted Western methodologies, epistemology, and hermeneutics. Holistic mission theology has been a good starting point for beginning a decolonization, but it is still alienated. It has not been intentionally decolonial. It has, almost habitually, utilized external elements that tend to break up elements in its attempt to contextualize the message of the gospel in the social/political/economic/theological spheres. It has lacked self-criticism. It has adopted a version of Eurocentric history that does not accurately reflect what really happened. Finally, it has reflected on the care of creation only tangentially.

A question arises: To what degree do colonialist paradigms continue to permeate our theology in Latin America? The Gospel Coalition (Coalición por el Evangelio) denies the gospel of Jesus Christ by claiming that it possesses the only true interpretation of it. It uses a methodology that claims to be universal without being contextualized. Therefore, it removes an essential foundation for the expansion of the kingdom of God. In other words, it again becomes colonialist. It comes from the (Global) North. It represents the most conservative evangelical and Calvinist groups, the most fundamentalist groups devoid of compassion, justice, or peace. Nevertheless, simultaneously, the riverbed of Western theology has representatives who, with tenacity, have turned their postulates toward a holistic understanding of life and the gospel message. John Stott and Christopher Wright are British theologians who have created new and different approaches to their work of reflection in dialogue with African, Asian, and Latin American colleagues.

Conclusion

Faced with this reality, I propose several concrete actions. I express my dissent by placing history in its appropriate place with adequate content. It is then necessary to act responsibly by inclusively tying together historical time and geopolitical space. For the same reason, it is important to keep together the life and history of peoples in relationship with their geographical territories, their cultural, economic, and religious factors.

Therefore, we need to create a new discernment, centered in the One who spilled his human blood, an act that did and will put an end to chaos, because history will be purified of its stains, and the ecosystem will renew its creative purpose and function in harmonious balance. What motivates us in this direction is that the descendant of the woman has crushed the head of his adversary.

Finally, our fundamental frame of reference continues to be Jesus. This foundation is vital to give meaning to the restoration of equilibrium. We are dealing with a Jesus who is challenging, powerful, and clothed in the gospel of the kingdom of God. This is the Jesus who is the incarnate truth, historically ecological, and solidly made known in the Scriptures. This way of seeing Jesus is key to directly experiencing his breath, his vital will, both in the written word and in the Word made flesh: in the Scriptures and in his person.

References

Arzans de Orsúa y Vela, Bartolomé. *El mundo desde Potosí: Vida y reflexiones de Bartolomé Arzans de Orsúa y Vela (1676–1736) – Selección, prólogo y notas de Mariano Baptista Gumucio*. Santa Cruz: Grupo Santander Central Hispano, 2000.

BioLogos. "Why Should Christians Care for Creation?" 7 December 2019. Accessed 10 September 2020. https://biologos.org/common-questions/why-should-christians-care-for-creation.

Comisión Episcopal de Pastoral Social Cáritas Bolivia. "Ricos y pobres: la brecha se ensancha." *Revista de Análisis Económico* vol. 19 (2004).

Dussel, Enrique. "Europa, Modernidad y Eurocentrismo." In *La colonialidad del saber: eurocentrismo y ciencias sociales – Perspectivas Latinoamericanas*, edited by Edgardo Lander, 24–33. Buenos Aires: CLACSO, 2000.

Galeano, Eduardo. *Las venas abiertas de América Latina*. Buenos Aires: Siglo Veintiuno, 2004.

Vilches, A., et al. "Biodiversidad." 2014. Accessed 3 September 2020. https://www.researchgate.net/publication/302790840_Biodiversidad.

———, et al. "Frenar el cambio climático." Online article. 2014. Accessed 10 September 2020. https://www.researchgate.net/publication/302295798_Frenar_el_Cambio_Climatico.

10

Outline of a Latin American Socioenvironmental Theology

Víctor Manuel Morales Vásquez

Theological reflection has, as its goal, to enable us to understand the world where we live in light of divine revelation. This unfolds throughout the length and breadth of the universe. As the psalmist says, "The heavens declare the glory of God; the skies proclaim the work of his hands" (Psalm 19:1). This kind of revelation is known as natural theology, which is subordinated to the specific and concrete revelation of the actions and covenants of the God of Israel, culminating with Jesus, the incarnate Word.[1]

This exercise in reflection should conclude with some ethical guidelines for redeemed moral agents, that is to say, the church. The goal is that the church will communicate and implement them in order to solve problems whose complexity highlights the need to integrate different and relevant ways of knowing for specific contexts. In the case we are addressing, we refer to the Latin American cultural mosaic.

This necessity to integrate different ways of knowing requires a framework and a unifying principle that will coordinate them. The resulting synergy constitutes a source of inspiration for the creation of initiatives that will foment a better quality of life for the communities that share the same biosphere.

In this chapter I aim to build precisely this kind of theological reflection. I will begin with a cursory glance at the critical situation of Latin American

---

[1]. It is good to acknowledge here the well-known theological dispute between Emil Brunner and Karl Barth regarding the two kinds of revelation. This theological disagreement has a particular impact upon any attempt to develop an environmental theology. See Emil Brunner and Karl Barth, *Natural Theology* (Eugene: Wipf and Stock, 2002).

ecosystems, giving a few examples. The problem of our ecological destruction and the issue of sustainable development constitute the topics of my reflection. Then I will describe the methodological framework that I will utilize for an analysis of the contributions that Latin American theologians and philosophers have made regarding these issues. Finally, I will conclude with an outline of an environmental theology with a Latin American flavor. It is important to point out that the evangelical church should contribute to this already existent synergy by paying attention to the mosaic made from the diverse disciplines and ways of knowing.

Through this exercise I highlight the need to know both the local and the global contexts of the problems and their interlocutors. I also argue that the evangelical church has the opportunity to make a significant contribution to the debate. This is because a true integration is possible only from the perspective of the gospel that places emphasis on the life, work, death, and resurrection of Jesus Christ, *Pantocrátor*, that is, the all-powerful God.

The Ecological Crisis and Sustainable Development: Some Examples from the Current Situation

Latin America presents severe cases of environmental problems. I will present just three examples that represent typical situations from the Latin American context. First, I will refer to the problem of criminality and attempts at biodiversity conservation. Second, I will address the political conflict between the private sector, farmers, and indigenous communities. Finally, I will mention the high pollution levels in Latin American cities. At the same time, I will underline the display of creativity shown by Latin American youth in their enthusiasm to provide workable solutions to the environmental challenges.

Monarch Butterflies in Mexico and the Illegal Cutting Down of Trees

Both organized crime and authorized corporative crime are the real obstacles to genuine attempts to develop conservation programs and environmental control. This involves resource utilization and exploitation through the use of power. The violence that ranges from threats to assassinations blunts initiatives to conserve areas destined for the protection of biodiversity. In Mexico, the area that constitutes the summer habitat of the monarch butterfly is threatened by the illegal cutting down of pines, cedars, poplars, elms, and other trees. Environmental activists have been killed for their attempts to protect such lands.² These acts are committed not only by groups of organized criminals but also by corporate groups, as I will describe in the next example.

The Destruction of the Amazon and the Indigenous Populations

Indigenous populations in the Amazon have suffered invasions of their lands due to the mineral and agricultural wealth they represent. Foreign and national corporations have received full authorization and support from the government. They justify this authorization on the grounds that it is necessary for the economic development of Brazil. The question is, which Brazil?

In addition, farmers claim it is necessary to expropriate indigenous lands in order to develop the agricultural potential in their hands. The use of violence exacerbates the already tense situation. Recently, there have been more assassinations, which has caused indigenous people to mobilize. This is in spite of the fact that their land rights are protected by the constitution.³

The High Pollution Levels in Cities and the Capacity for Invention

Mexico City has been characterized as having elevated levels of pollution. For decades, attempts have been made to implement measures to reduce the level of particles per million (ppm) of pollution agents in the air to acceptable levels prescribed by the World Health Organization. In the city there are more than 5,500,000 vehicles.

In response to this need, there are young people, for example, who dream of changing used gasoline cars into electric cars with a price tag that is acceptable to many drivers. Beyond a culture of improvisation, these young adults are offering their professional services. In particular, their work is adaptable to the specific needs of each case.⁴ Sadly, they are doing this without any federal support.

---

2. For example, see BBC News, "Homero Gómez: Missing Mexican Butterfly Activist Found Dead," 30 January 2020, accessed 3 August 2020, https://www.bbc.com/news/world-latin-america-51304857.

3. For example, see BBC News, "Brazil's Indigenous People: Miners Kill One in Invasion of Protected Reserve," 28 July 2019, accessed 3 August 2020, https://www.bbc.com/news/world-latin-america-49144917.

4. For example, see BBC News, "Mexico City Pollution: Residents Urged to Stay Indoors," 15 May 2019, accessed 3 August 2020, https://www.bbc.com/news/world-latin-america-48279872.

The Gospel, the Dialogue of Ways of Knowing, and Civil Society

This situation illustrates an advance in awareness of the environmental problem while at the same time it promotes a creativity that is needed to deal with new situations. This confirms what Plato affirmed: necessity is the mother of invention.

All these cases demonstrate unusual aspects of the environmental problems in our countries. It is a mosaic of conflicting interests of great importance with a high degree of complexity. It is clear that we need to encourage dialogue between advocates for the different disciplines and ways of knowing. Theologians, philosophers, and scientists need to exchange their points of view with the goal of better understanding the nature of the challenges, and to seek short-term, midterm, and long-range solutions. It is not enough for the experts to dialogue. They also need to acknowledge themselves as members of civil society.

I propose that, in particular, Latin American evangelical Christians seek to influence the court of public opinion at local, national, and international levels. The first step to take in this direction is to recognize ourselves as part of this public space. The second step will occur when we realize that the gospel is holistic. The gospel's reach has cosmic dimensions. We affirm this every time we quote John 3:16. Nevertheless, we seldom pause to reflect on the word "world." This is the object of the love of God the Father through his Son Jesus Christ.

Holistic Vision and Redemption History

This chapter has as its goal to challenge readers to think holistically about the reach of the gospel that we believe and proclaim in Latin America. I begin with the fact that, in general, the majority of evangelicals have a vision of the world that is segmented and compartmentalized. There are very few who have understood that the mission we have been given is to the world, in general. In Mark 16:15 there is another reference to the *cosmos*, that is, the world. The individual, as such, is an invention of modernity. Our challenge is to recover a cosmology, that is, a way to understand reality. This must go beyond the liberal concept of the centrality of the individual. We need a cosmology that considers all of life.

Based on this perspective, I propose that we begin by approaching the topic by looking at narrative as a heuristic concept, that is, as a frame of reference to configure holistic visions of the world that lead to relevant and contextualized ethical guidelines. The reason for this is that everyone's identity is rooted in a narrative which is the foundation for the way each person makes his or her decisions.⁵ In other words, this is ethics. In this case, this will be the methodological basis for the development of an environmental theology *from* Latin America and *for* Latin America.

First, I would like to respond to the challenge that Lynn White posed in the 1960s. A growing theological and philosophical corpus emerged and created awareness of the negative effects that had resulted from a particular interpretation of Genesis 1:26. This interpretation authorized humanity to exploit creation, which came to be reduced to the status of a natural resource, or natural capital. Obviously, this accusation is not the whole story, because it leaves along the wayside a vision of modernity as expressed by Francis Bacon, one of its principal ideologues. Both interpretations would hand over the baton of cultural leadership from Christianity to modernity. The first stage would entrust the so-called "cultural mandate," the theological foundation for the dominion of the earth, to the stage that followed it, the philosophical "instrumental rationality" that is a fusion of science with technology.

Nevertheless, Lynn White placed the emphasis on another foundational aspect that uses to be omitted in the discussion, namely, the primordial role of beliefs: "Human ecology is deeply conditioned by beliefs about our nature and destiny, that is, by religion."⁶

Lynn White maintained that the ecological crisis had its roots in the religious character of every cosmology.⁷ Therefore, it is indispensable for us to first explore and clarify which beliefs and convictions are the most deeply rooted in our hearts, as a symbol of our existence.⁸ This exploratory journey will place us in the right condition for being able to achieve a holistic understanding of the environmental problem. We will later build a sufficiently robust worldview for the type of transformation we want to introduce into our way of life as a guide for a narrative which will add color and texture to our existence.

---

5. The relationship between the concepts of identity and narrative are the principal theme in the writings of Protestant philosopher Paul Ricoeur, *Soi-même comme un autre* (Paris: Seuil, 1990).

6. Lynn White, "Appendix I: The Historical Roots of our Ecologic Crisis," in *Pollution and the Death of Man: The Christian View of Ecology*, ed. Francis Schaeffer (London: Hodder and Stoughton, 1970), 78.

7. Lynn White stated: "Given that the roots of our problem are essentially religious, the remedy should also be essentially religious, whether we identify it as such or not. We need to rethink and reflect on our nature and destiny." White, "Appendix I," 85.

8. The use of the "heart" as a symbol of our existence dates back to St. Augustine in his *Confessions*.

For this reason, I propose redemption history as the theological and historical basis, and narrative as the foundation for an integrating worldview that will permit the formulation of an environmental theology with a Latin American flavor. To that end, I will clarify the dimensions of that history. I will then let that history enter into dialogue with the theological heuristic of the Argentine Pope Francis and with the philosophical heuristic of the Mexican Enrique Leff.[9]

This scientific exercise has as its goal to provide an example of how different ways of knowing can come together. I will refer to this throughout this chapter. It is necessary to pay attention to the proposals of other Latin Americans with whom we evangelicals should enter into dialogue. In this way, we will really be able to establish a common identity in the context of public opinion at local, national, and regional levels that cross the different sectors of society. Only in this way will we really communicate and have influence in the making of decisions. Our proposal will be relevant and pertinent because it emerges from within and not from an external imposition.

Regarding the beginning of the concept of redemption history, it is important to mention the work of theologians such as Oscar Cullmann and Herman Ridderbos, and of philosophers such as Karl Löwith, who proposed the concept of salvation as the development of the plot of a story. If we were to simplify such a story by using structural analysis categories for any narrative, we would begin with creation as the initial situation. Then would come the conflict of the fall into sin. We would then pass through redemption by Jesus Christ as the resolution of the conflict. We would then conclude with the new creation as the ending, that is, a transformed state. Such a narrative constitutes the history of the cosmos, that is, of life. This transcendental aspect becomes necessary in order to guarantee the *facticity* of a holistic worldview that is illuminated by theological reflection on the problem of the environmental crisis from the perspective of the gospel rooted in the soil of Latin America.[10]

I propose interaction and dialogue with other Latin American holistic proposals that constitute this Latin American soil that we are a part of. The relevance of the message that we Latin American evangelicals share is guaranteed through a larger understanding of the real problems and proposals made by them.

---

9. The concept of "heuristic" refers to a *methodological outline* that guides the search for a solution to the problem.

10. Here "facticity" has the meaning of what will become an overwhelming fact and not something that remains just a mere possibility.

At the same time, we should expect the same kind of openness from these other interlocutors. In this way, a better Latin American understanding of our environment will develop. As we stand on this foundation of interaction, we open up the possibility of a critical understanding of the most important elements by all the participants of our large Latin American community.

From Latin America and for Latin America: Other Perspectives

The Uruguayan Catholic theologian Guillermo Kerber describes in his doctoral dissertation particular aspects of a Latin American ecological theology. This theological proposal is a scientific task oriented toward action under the guidelines of an ethic for the whole of life. It strives to delineate a social ecology that understands the variety of crises as different faces of the same phenomenon.[11] It does not try to consider the environmental crisis, the economic crisis, and the cultural and political crisis in isolation. It warns us that we are face to face with a general crisis that brings together all of these aspects, and it strives to find equally holistic solutions.

The Encyclical "Laudato Si'" of Pope Francis: Toward a Holistic Ecology

Although the encyclical is a collegial product, Pope Francis has left his personal mark on this document which reflects the particular concerns of his Latin American world.[12] The text that addresses the current ecological crisis and the issue of sustainable development has the benefit of being able to be read by multiple groups beyond the Roman Catholic community.

Francis proposes a holistic ecology that brings together the field of environmental ecology and an ecology that is concerned with the social dimension. Such a holistic ecology is based on a fact of a reticular character. This means that our existence is connected to the existence of other creatures and the same spatial/temporal conditions for life. It is imperative that we overcome a false dichotomy that pits humans against an amorphous world that they can exploit at their will. This separatist vision considers humans as diametrically opposed to nature and its environment, but also pits humans

---

11. Guillermo Kerber, *O ecológico e a teología latino-americana: Articulação e desafíos* (Porto Alegre: Conselho Mundial de Igrejas, 2006), 84.

12. Pope Francis, "Encyclical Letter *Laudato Si'* of the Holy Father Francis on Care for Our Common Home," 24 May 2015, https://www.vatican.va/content/francesco/en/encyclicals/documents/papa-francesco_20150524_enciclica-laudato-si.html.

against other human beings. In order to address and resolve the general crisis, we need to set aside any strategy that objectifies and transforms nature into a resource and other humans into an instrument or means to an end. The immediate consequence of such an objectifying and instrumentalist practice is the loss of the intrinsic value of people and their environment. Logically speaking, a utilitarian approach is presented as if it were the only option.

The encyclical begins with the fact that the world is a divine gift, just as it is expressed in Genesis. Pope Francis's reading of Genesis puts emphasis on human labor as the central element of human cultural activity. The human was placed in a reworked, designed space – to be more precise, a garden. For this reason, the pope recognizes that the best way to preserve creation is to work it with the objective of developing its potentialities. Work has as its goal the transformation of creation, restricted only by the parameter that such transformation be according to the order established by the Creator for each creature.

The environment being understood as the interaction and the interdependence between human beings and their surroundings opens the possibility for a true, sustainable, and viable development given the parameters that the same environmental and human reality dictates. We cannot live in a perpetual state of destruction without annihilating ourselves in the process. The place where each community finds itself provides color and texture to that community's way of life. Therefore, according to Francis, the loss of the cultural inheritance of each people group is even worse than the loss of biodiversity. The growing extinction of cultural universes can be compared to the irreparable extinction of plant and animal species. The homogenizing processes imposed by the economic phenomenon of globalization end with the erosion of the rich cultural terrain and transform it into a "nonplace."[13] Such nonplaces are the result of true culture wars where the losers, faced with a fierce battle, end up by giving in and adopting alienating patterns of behavior.

This cultural section is highlighted in the encyclical, which also dedicates a lot of space to socioenvironmental poverty in the cities. Pope Francis exhorts us to create spaces of hope. Urban overcrowding represents a true socioenvironmental problem. It is necessary here to rethink the urban dynamic of how city inhabitants can live in a dignified manner. Spaces of hope

---

13. This is an anthropological concept that Marc Auge explains in his book that carries the same name, *Los no lugares, espacios de anonimato: Una antropología de la sobremodernidad* (Barcelona: Gedisa, 2007). These are spaces without local identity because their color and texture have disappeared as a result of the uniformity brought about by globalization.

should lead to greater social contact to lessen the degradation of the natural environment. We need to have green spaces that invite positive coexistence and a sense of belonging to a community. In other words, it becomes necessary to create socioenvironmental conditions that lead to the formation of local cultural identity.

Finally, we need to point out a revisioning of technology in our lives. The pope launches a criticism of what he calls the technological paradigm. He begins with the fact that technology is a gift from God. This divine gift is indispensable to achieve the legitimate human goals of transforming our environment. Nevertheless, it is equally urgent to redirect the kind of technological development that posits human beings as the maximum goal. As a result of having merely mercantilist objectives, it becomes justified to reduce human beings to the status of throwaway material together with the environment which is also considered to be disposable. In contrast, a moral ecology will have the common good as a framework. The encyclical holds to an ethic based on the common good and distributive justice. In this way, we can evaluate not only economic and political paradigms, but also cultural and social ones that govern how local, national, and international programs are conceived. The encyclical gives special attention to the problem not only of intergenerational poverty but also intragenerational poverty. It highlights the importance of creating a world by following these criteria: a sustainable world under the rule of a holistic ecology.

The challenge of creating a different world is a project that demands the creativity of all of society's sectors. There must be a genuine concern for poor people today and in the future. As I have already mentioned, poverty is not just economical, but also socioenvironmental. There will always be vulnerable sectors that will require our attention. Solutions to these challenges that arise will be effective and viable only within a framework that is sufficiently large so as to capture the complexity of the relations that characterize our environment.[14]

---

14. For more details regarding this analysis, see Enrique Figueroa Clemente, *La ecología del papa Francisco: un mensaje para un planeta y un mundo en crisis – Reflexiones ecológicas sobre la Carta encíclica "Laudato Sí" sobre el cuidado de la casa común* (Madrid: Biblioteca de Autores Cristianos, 2016).

Enrique Leff: For an Environmental Rationality

I now move to comment on the holistic worldview of the Mexican philosopher Enrique Leff.[15] Environmental rationality functions as a conceptual guiding principle in his work, which is in tune with the revolutionary zeitgeist (the spirit of the age) of Latin America in the twentieth century. Nevertheless, instead of borrowing from the work of Karl Marx, Enrique Leff appropriates, in particular, the philosophy of Martin Heidegger. He also borrows from several postmodern philosophers for whom the deconstruction of the discourse of modernity became the primary objective of their work.

Leff's objective is not limited to deconstructing concepts. In addition, he proposes to project a world that is different because it is sustainable. His deconstruction has a retrospective aspect, that is, he directs his gaze toward a disorganized state of things. In other words, he observes the entropy that is characteristic of the environmental crisis. His scientific project asks what the basic causes of this metaphysical order are; that is to say, he proposes going to the heart of existence itself. From there he moves to establish the foundations for the reconstruction of the world. This is the prospective element of his philosophical endeavor. To this end, he takes advantage of the conceptual apparatus and elements of the existentialist philosophy of Heidegger, for whom humanity's basic problem was precisely the oblivion of being. At the root of the ecological crisis we find the essential problem of being that will lead to a resolution that will permit an emergence of a sustainable world that has life itself as its priority.

Leff identifies the so-called "instrumental rationality" as the cause of the increasing disorderly state of things that will result in even greater imbalances. Regarding Latin America, he warns that the implementation of mercantilist economic policies has created a cultural and social homogenization that has erased the unique identities of each region. This is leading to the deconstruction of the discourses of instrumental rationality within the framework of an environmental rationality which proposes a reconfiguration of the world interpreted from the viewpoint of the *physis*,[16] in other words, life. Following

---

15. This segment is essentially a reflection on the thinking of Enrique Leff in *Saber Ambiental: sustentabilidad, racionalidad, complejidad, poder* (Mexico City: Siglo Veintiuno, 1998); *Aventuras de la epistemología ambiental Veintiuno* (Mexico City: Siglo Veintiuno, 2006); *El fuego de la vida: Heidegger ante la cuestión ambiental* (Mexico City: Siglo Veintiuno, 2018).

16. The word *physis* is the Greek word for nature.

the goals of the logocentric critique typical of postmodern schools,[17] Leff clarifies that the heart of the environmental crises is lived out in a struggle between the *logos* and the *physis*. *Logos* has won this battle because it has known how to impose upon the vital impulses of the *physis* a separation between what is real (*physis*) and what is symbolic (*logos*). The effects have been destructive. It has created a situation in which violence is justified as the vehicle needed to achieve the system's stability.

As has already been stated, this dichotomy leads to a growing division between nature and society. Environmental rationality brings together within the concept of environment the history of the ways in which societies have interacted with the environment. This produces knowledge and helps them to forge their own identities. In other words, environmental rationality can be defined as the appropriation of nature by society. It is the social interpretation of a region about its environment. This interpretation presupposes a multiplicity of ways of knowing.

Appealing to the existential philosophy of Heidegger, Leff highlights the particular and concrete situation of *being-there*, that is, of *Dasein*. We need to remember that Heidegger proposed rewriting the history of being, that is, he wanted to produce a different ontology, a different understanding of being as existence and not as essence. The latter would be predetermined whereas the ontology of existence would be conceived as a project, given that human beings are thrown into the world with the obligation to forge an existence, that is, an identity.

Both the criticism leveled at logocentrism as well as the notion of a new ontology are transformed into the metaphysical foundations that Leff believes are necessary to be able to articulate new worlds and new ways of living that are characterized by being sustainable. Environmental rationality celebrates both difference and complexity. It is committed to change and to the transformation of people, beginning with their ties to their homeland. Only in this way can we face the logic of uniformity of instrumental rationality imposed by market economies, the political policies that they encourage, and the juridical body that protects them.

---

17. Logocentrism is the philosophical posture that gives priority to the word (*logos*) and to the idea of a concept that imposes closure on other interpretations that are essentially subversive. This subversion manifests itself most powerfully through words. Jacques Derrida, promotor of deconstruction as a philosophical strategy, coined the neologism *différance*, distinguishing it from *différence* to demonstrate the subversive nature of words. This latter French word means "difference."

Toward an Environmental Theology

For Roger Garaudy as well as for Lynn White, the environmental crisis also had a religious root. The center of our existence, that is, our heart, does not find genuine rest because God is not that center of our existence. Instead of rest, we encounter violence. The satisfaction of the idols is based upon the extinction of life itself, "the growth of the hidden god of our societies, the cruel god that demands human sacrifices, and that puts in doubt the survival of the planet and those who inhabit it."[18]

Garaudy added that the widespread suffering is due to the fact that the world has lost its way. Mercantilist goals will never be able to provide abundant, full, and holistic satisfaction for humanity. Thanks to the ecological crisis, human beings have realized their limitations and the problem of confusing growth with development.

> We suffer because we live in a world without an end goal. In relationship with economic growth, it manifested that it is not true that economic growth permits us to face crises. To the contrary, it creates crises because it leads to an ever-increasing unequal distribution of power and privileges.[19]

I maintain with Pope Francis and with Leff that we must first recognize that the unsustainable present is a product of a past that had utilitarian and instrumental objectives that later pushed us to think about a sustainable future. This is the task that we Latin Americans have before us. To achieve this, we need to encourage a dialogue that appreciates and appropriates in a critical way the task of laying the foundations of an environmental theology that contributes to building that new world. We evangelicals need to get rid of every dichotomy that undervalues daily affairs. We need to acknowledge the truth of the history of redemption and our place in it as agents of the kingdom of God. We should affirm the active presence of the trinitarian God through the person of the Holy Spirit. This Spirit is transforming the world and the history of the world toward a specific, concrete end, which is the fullness of the redemption of all things by God the Father through his Son. This historical dimension constitutes the much larger frame of reference and the strongest foundation for a genuine transformation.

---

18. Roger Garaudy, *Una nueva civilización: El Proyecto Esperanza* (Madrid: Cuadernos para el Diálogo, 1977); quoted in Figueroa Clemente, *La ecología del papa Francisco*, 147.

19. Garaudy, quoted in Figueroa Clemente, *La ecología del papa Francisco*, 147.

Conclusion

As we can see, Leff's proposal lines up well with the intention of the encyclical "*Laudato Si*." They both develop a concept of ecology that emerges from the interdependence between society and nature. Latin America, with its problems of injustice and social inequalities, as well as its growing ecological crisis, gives a local tone to the project of developing an environmental theology. We evangelicals must not let the opportunity slip by to make real the truth of God's salvific acts in history. The socioenvironmental crisis requires holistic solutions that imply a genuine *metanoia*. This repentance cannot be reduced to a mere change of mind or be understood as just a change of paradigm. Real repentance needs to go deeper and reach the roots of our existence.

The history of redemption is the history of the evangelical people. It provides the maximum identity together with local color and flavor. An environmental theology such as the one I have sketched requires a guiding principle that brings together every sphere of life. We are faced, therefore, with the responsibility of interpreting the socioenvironmental crisis in light of the history of redemption, that is, the history of God the creator and redeemer of his people and of the world. The challenges of the twenty-first century are a window of opportunity to project a sustainable world lined up with the kingdom of God.

References

Auge, Marc. *Los no lugares, espacios de anonimato: Una antropología de la sobremodernidad*. Barcelona: Gedisa, 2007.

BBC News. "Brazil's Indigenous People: Miners Kill One in Invasion of Protected Reserve." 28 July 2019. Accessed 3 August 2020. https://www.bbc.com/news/world-latin-america-49144917.

———. "Homero Gómez: Missing Mexican Butterfly Activist Found Dead." 30 January 2020. Accessed 3 August 2020. https://www.bbc.com/news/world-latin-america-51304857.

———. "Mexico City Pollution: Residents Urged to Stay Indoors." 15 May 2019. Accessed 3 August 2020. https://www.bbc.com/news/world-latin-america-48279972.

Brunner, Emil, and Karl Barth. *Natural Theology*. Eugene: Wipf and Stock, 2002.

Figueroa Clemente, Enrique. *La ecología del papa Francisco: un mensaje para un planeta y un mundo en crisis – Reflexiones ecológicas sobre la Carta encíclica "Laudato Si" sobre el cuidado de la casa común*. Madrid: Biblioteca de Autores Cristianos, 2016.

Garaudy, Roger. *Una nueva civilización: El Proyecto Esperanza*. Madrid: Cuadernos para el Diálogo, 1977.

Kerber, Guillermo. *O ecológico e a teología latino-americana: Articulação e desafíos*. Porto Alegre: Conselho Mundial de Igrejas, 2006.

Leff, Enrique. *Aventuras de la epistemología ambiental Veintiuno*. Mexico City: Siglo Veintiuno, 2006.

———. *El fuego de la vida: Heidegger ante la cuestión ambiental*. Mexico City: Siglo Veintiuno, 2018.

———. *Saber Ambiental: sustentabilidad, racionalidad, complejidad, poder*. Mexico City: Siglo Veintiuno, 1998.

Pope Francis. "Encyclical Letter *Laudato Si'* of the Holy Father Francis on Care for Our Common Home." 24 May 2015. https://www.vatican.va/content/francesco/en/encyclicals/documents/papa-francesco_20150524_enciclica-laudato-si.html.

Ricoeur, Paul. *Soi-même comme un autre*. Paris: Seuil, 1990.

White, Lynn. "Appendix I: The Historical Roots of our Ecological Crisis." In *Pollution and the Death of Man: The Christian View of Ecology*, edited by Francis Schaeffer. London: Hodder and Stoughton, 1970.

11

The Discernment Community as a Paradigm for a Continuing Reformation

Rafael Zaracho

Every year, to a greater or lesser degree, we remember and celebrate the Reformation. Nevertheless, *what* we remember, and more than anything else, *how* we celebrate the Reformation, becomes especially challenging, keeping in mind my faith tradition, which is Anabaptist, and especially my location, Latin America. My faith tradition and geographical region have something in common: both are considered to be on the periphery. I will use the concept of "periphery" as it is used by Juan Driver to delineate my proposals for answering the questions of what to remember and how to celebrate the Reformation. In light of the concept of periphery, I propose and invite my readers to see, on the one hand, those circles of discernment or communities of faith as "accents" of the Spirit. In addition, I present our community theologies or reflections as "faithful attempts" under the guidance of the Spirit. In brief, I am inviting you to consider discernment communities as a paradigmatic element and space for the continual reformation or *ecclesia reformata, reformanda secundum verbum Dei* and through the discernment communities.[1]

---

1. Ecclesia reformata, reformanda secundum verbum Dei: the church reformed, always reforming according to the word of God.

The Periphery and Discernment Spaces

In recent years, the concept of periphery has come to be used to refer to a theology that is lived and forged in and from the Majority World.[2] Juan Driver proposes a rereading of the history of Christianity that places emphasis on the marginalized, the minority faith communities, heretics, and those relegated to the margins of official religion. These groups had a peripheral existence in the distinct moments of history. For a reading of history, Driver proposes starting with a biblical vision of history that is rooted in the pilgrimage of the people of God. Beginning with the call, formation, and pilgrimage of the people of Israel in the Old Testament and the formation of the messianic people in the New Testament (the gospels and the Pauline and Petrine letters), we can affirm that the "biblical history of the people of God is . . . the history of this people at the service of the kingdom . . . a kingdom characterized by God's predilection for the marginalized."[3] The peripheral nature of these faith communities and their members, present both in the Old Testament and in the New, lasted from the first centuries until the time of Constantine. This began a process in which the church went from being a persecuted minority to become recognized and protected by the secular power.

According to Driver, these periphery movements of faith within the history of Christianity, from the first century until our times, present certain common characteristics. First, there is a notorious "solidarity with the marginalized." Second, there is a renunciation of political power where (a) even in the midst of persecutions "they continued to practice their non-violence vision," (b) they generally questioned the alliance of the church with the state, and (c) "they have offered a powerful prophetic protest against the coercion designed to maintain social peace at all costs, both in the church and in society." Third, they understood and lived with a "sense of vocation to the messianic vision in the world" made manifest in (a) *communities* that stood in contrast and as alternatives to the models in society, and (b) movements of *evangelization* in word and deed, and (c) they frequently died as *martyrs* in the process of

---

2. This emphasis and dimension of theology represents the third theological movement of the twentieth century, according to Gibellini, which seeks to connect and assume a theological praxis with a political conscience. Within this third movement are the theologies of the Majority World, black theology in the United States, feminist theology, etc. The first two movements were "led" by Barth (dialectic theology) and Bultmann (existential theology). The fourth is a theology that has an ecumenical and planetary conscience and emphasis. R. Gibellini, *La teología del siglo XX* (Santander: SAL TERRAE, 1998), 554.

3. Juan Driver, *La fe en la periferia de la historia: Una historia del pueblo cristiano desde la perspectiva de los movimientos de restauración y reforma radical* (Guatemala: CLARA-Semilla, 1997), 43.

communicating the grace of the gospel. A common element that motivated, inspired, oriented, and determined the agenda of these communities, continues Driver, was "the biblical vision and expectation of the kingdom of God."[4]

I am going to use the word "periphery" following Driver's proposal: that is, a theology that is forged, thought, made, and lived *in* and *from* the periphery has at least the following general characteristics. First, it will be a reflection that is forged, thought, made, and lived in and from a deep *solidarity* with those who are marginalized by political, social, and religious structures. Second, it will be a community reflection characterized by a clear awareness of the nature of discernment circles that gives these communities their character of being the Spirit's "accent." In the third place, it will be a reflection that seeks to create and support dynamic community spaces and in which these efforts are seen as "faithful attempts" under the guidance of the Spirit. The periphery, more than a virtue per se, is an attitude and willingness for vulnerability and interdependence to search for and be guided by the Spirit as members of our faith communities in light of our rich biblical, historical, and religious tradition.[5] Therefore, my focus, rather than describing in detail the steps necessary for establishing a theological paradigm, will be to concentrate on the need to create safe spaces for discernment. In other words, I will propose how in and through these discernment spaces we can encourage and sustain the emphases that these periphery communities have maintained. In addition, through these discernment communities, we can remember, celebrate, and recover the spirit of the Reformation movement. This means seeing how to realign our beliefs and practices in light of the good news of the gospel of Jesus Christ.

Ecclesia Discens and *Ecclesia Docens*

We can celebrate and remember the Reformation when, first, as members of our faith communities and in light of the religious Reformation of the sixteenth century, our theological reflection seeks to be forged, lived, and thought *in*

---

4. Driver, *La fe en la periferia de la historia*, 293–94.
5. See, for example, the chapters of Enrique Dussel and Rubem Alves that offer a good panoramic summary of the origin, development, and challenges of theology in our continent up to 1980: Enrique Dussel, "Hipótesis para una historia de la teología en América Latina (1492–1980)," in *Materiales para una teología en América Latina*, ed. Pablo Richard (San José: DEI, 1980), 401–52; Rubem Alves, "Las ideas teológicas y sus caminos por los surcos institucionales del protestantismo brasileño," in Richard, *Materiales para una teología en América Latina*, 343–66.

and *from* a deep *solidarity* with those marginalized by political, social, and religious structures. As individuals and as communities we deliberately strive to be an *ecclesia discens* – that is, a community of faith that as its first act of obedience to God *listens* both to Scripture and to the needs and cries of those who are in the periphery. Jon Sobrino reminds us that those who have been marginalized generally have less access and fewer ways to make other people aware of their concerns and needs. Therefore, in this constant and continuing effort for the "fusion of horizons" (*Horizontsverschmelzung*) we try to take the place and point of view of the needy and of those who are on the periphery.⁶ In this dynamic and ongoing process we need to renew and reevaluate our commitment to give recognition to the presence of the needy and marginalized in light of the good news of the gospel.⁷ The words of Calvin, cited by Barth, "*Omnis recta cognitio Dei ab oboedentia nascitur*," or the "true knowledge of God is born out of obedience," help us to realign our practices and convictions.⁸ In just a few words, a theological reflection that is lived in and from the periphery will be seen as an ongoing activity of an *ecclesia discens* that renews its missional commitment to live, walk, and reflect in and from the marginalized or those on the periphery. This is possible because the members of this community see the purpose and nature of their existence in light of the kingdom of God and are guided by the dynamic notion of a community sojourn that gives them an openness to evaluate and discern their knowledge and experiences and will permit them to be guided by the Spirit.⁹

To the degree that we are an *ecclesia discens* of Scripture and of the people who live at the margins of society we will be able to fulfill our prophetic role

---

6. Jon Sobrino, *Christ the Liberator: A View from the Victims* (Maryknoll: Orbis, 2001), 7.

7. Nordstokke, referring to Luther's Ninety-Five Theses and identifying them as a form of struggle against the abuses of religious power, says, "The defense of causes is not the same as lobbying which is trying to influence governments or other leaders in order to benefit one's own interests or those of an organization. This defense is concerned, first of all, with the marginalized groups of the church or society who cannot defend themselves or who are silenced for various reasons. This does not mean that the defense of causes speaks in the place of others or ignores the voice of those it is claiming to defend. To the contrary, the defense of causes presupposes listening and being in solidarity." K. Nordstokke, "La iglesia y el espacio político: una interpretación luterana," in *Libres por la gracia de Dios*, ed. A. Burghardt (Geneva: La Federación Luterana Mundial, 2016), 36.

8. Karl Barth, "The Place of Theology," in *Theological Foundations for Ministry*, ed. R. Anderson (Edinburgh: T&T Clark, 1979), 31.

9. Regarding these affirmations, see Gerhard Lowfink, *Jesus and Community: The Social Dimension of Christian Faith* (Philadelphia: Fortress, 1984), 31–32; Robert J. Banks, *Paul's Idea of Community: The Early House Churches in Their Cultural Setting* (Peabody: Hendrickson, 1994), 47–48; Jack Suderman, *Re-Imagining the Church: Implications of Being a People in the World* (Eugene: Wipf and Stock, 2016), 71–89.

of being an *ecclesia docens*. This is a community of faith that *teaches* as a faithful witness, in words and deeds, the saving works of God. The quality and faithfulness of an *ecclesia docens* will be able to be evaluated and measured to the degree to which it promotes the vision and expectations of the kingdom of God inaugurated by Jesus Christ. This community of faith nourishes its hope and its daily practice in light of the life, ministry, death, and resurrection of its Lord and Savior, Jesus Christ. Walking with our Lord was characterized by walking in mercy: "the rule of life of his disciples . . . would give first place to mercy."[10] With the goal of being a community of faith that renews its missional commitment to live, walk, and reflect in and from the periphery, we need to encourage communities of discernment.

Accents of the Spirit: Communities of Discernment

We can remember and celebrate the Reformation, second, when we work to become communities of discernment. These communities or circles of discernment speak of creative and imaginative processes in and through which we commit ourselves as disciples to name, distinguish, celebrate, and preserve relationships with God, with our brothers and sisters in the faith, and with the rest of creation. In these communities or spaces of discernment we seek to honor each participant, and no one automatically has the "final word." These spaces of discernment (i.e. groups that meet in homes, or national or regional conferences) have the communitarian accent of knowing, experiencing, and following Jesus. It is essential to create spaces for reflection and discernment on the dynamic between our knowing and following Jesus in our social, cultural, and religious spaces which frequently have perpetuated contexts of dehumanization. By "contexts of dehumanization" I have in mind the high levels of corruption, injustice, and poverty that are present in many parts of our countries. Our faith communities can be strengthened in safe spaces that honor the circles of discernment in and through which we follow and know Jesus. I propose two steps to help our communities of discernment.

Memory and Tradition: The Dynamic between Questions and Answers

Remembering is an act of recognition and appreciation for those who have gone before us in other times and places. In the biblical sense, remembering

---

10. Pope Francis, *Misericordia vultus: Bula de convocación del jubileo extraordinario de misericordia* (Asuncion: Paulinas HSP, 2016), 30.

is recognizing the presence, care, and faithfulness of God to a person, family, and community. It has tones and aspects of both celebration and warning. The festivals and sacred times in the Old Testament are a good example of this double dimension of remembering.[11] This brings us hope regarding the presence and faithfulness of God. At the same time, we are invited to review and evaluate our walk with God in the light of those who have gone before us.

I would suggest, as the first step, that the dynamic between questions and answers is fundamental for evaluating and appreciating aspects of our community memory and denominational tradition. As members of a specific denomination, the dynamic between questions and answers helps us to be aware of those theological or ethical aspects that we emphasize, ignore, or retain. This dynamic helps us to appreciate those questions and answers which we will emphasize, ignore, reject, or accept in and through our community and denominational spaces (examples: the ordination of women, the Holy Spirit, miracles, community, etc.). The invitation is to place the dynamic between questions and answers in the context of the discernment circles within our community and theological traditions. As we reflect upon the priorities of our questions and answers (or the dynamic between our knowing and our obeying), we might realize that some of our concerns and "current" answers (whether they be ethical, theological, doctrinal, or institutional) have been influenced by rich historical connections (for example, the Donatist controversy or the *filioque* debate). Other "concerns" have been shaped by the particularities of our contexts or have been "imported" to our region (e.g. the influence of premillennial dispensationalism in Latin America).[12] As we closely connect the dynamic between questions and answers, we can more easily appreciate the central role of discernment communities in forging, shaping, and preserving the community and theological emphases that we have inherited. The first step in becoming a community of discernment is *connecting* the historical and theological emphases of our faith communities and of the "culture" of our institutions in a close relationship in the dynamic between questions and answers.

---

11. William Dyrness, *Temas de la teología del Antiguo Testamento* (Miami: Vida, 1989), 110–24.

12. Daniel Salinas, *Taking up the Mantle: Latin American Evangelical Theology in the 20th Century* (Carlisle: Langham Global Library, 2017), 28.

Communities of Faith and Institutions as Accents of the Spirit

The second step in becoming discernment communities is to see the historical and theological emphases of our faith communities and institutions as "accents" of the Spirit.[13] The image of "accents" suggests the central place it occupies in our communities of faith. It is that in and through which we name, prioritize, celebrate, and preserve the dimensions of our relationships with our God, with our brothers and sisters, and with our contexts. Seeing our historical and theological emphases as "accents" of the Spirit can help us honor how our distinct communities and theological institutions have tried to be faithful to the kingdom of God in various times and cultures. In addition, this invites us to evaluate our own theological emphases and those of others in light of our reading of the Scriptures in our contexts (local, regional, and national) to the degree that we seek to be transformed into discernment communities guided by the Spirit.

Looking at our historical and theological emphases (and those of others) as accents of the Spirit calls us to be communities of discernment in which we honestly explore the flow and consequences of our beliefs and actions. In this process we seek to be faithful to the "heart of the gospel and not [only to] doctrinal accents."[14] We are invited to evaluate and judge the diversity of our faith communities and institutions regarding their quality of life and for their promotion of a reconciled creation. The implication is that we recognize and honor the "shame of the particularity" of the theological emphases and distinctives of our denominations and institutions.[15] These steps are possible to the degree that we retain the character and spirit of the periphery in our communities by not associating with coercive and manipulative authorities. In addition, we need to avoid all alliances that go against the essence of the gospel (see the section "*Ecclesia Discens* and *Ecclesia Docens*" above).

Memory and Tradition: Celebration and Repentance

In the process of promoting and growing in consciousness about our identity and accents, it is important to acknowledge the partial nature of our task of believing, discerning, celebrating, and mediating the presence of God in and

---

13. As part of my doctoral dissertation, I developed the idea of "accents" of the Spirit. See Rafael Zaracho, "The Role of Preferences in the Context of Believing and Discerning Communities: A Maturanian Reading" (PhD diss., University of St. Andrews, 2014).

14. Pope Francis, *Evangelii Gaudium* (Asuncion: Paulinas, HSP, 2013), 31.

15. John D. Roth, *Teaching That Transforms: Why Anabaptist-Mennonite Education Matters* (Scottsdale: Herald, 2011), 67.

through our experiences in the world. Under this point it is crucial to see the historical-theological differences of our varying institutions as "accents" of the Spirit. This concept of the "accents" of the Spirit will permit us to recognize how the Spirit has been, and still is, working in and through our faith communities (and those of others). Therefore, we can share with others the gifts of the Spirit that have been present in and through our own communities of discernment, and we will be open to learn from other communities that strive to be transformed into *ecclesia discens* and *ecclesia docens* under the leading of the Spirit. It is precisely in the context of our discernment communities that we can appreciate and evaluate those theological and ethical aspects that we have prioritized, ignored, or preserved in our faithful attempt to mediate, name, and celebrate the work and presence of God in our midst and in the world.

In the context of celebrating the Reformation, we can create spaces of evaluation of the denominational and institutional responses, and we may be able to arrive at *celebrating*, on the one hand, the success of the responses that have been given through the various circles of discernment over the years. This process of evaluation could also lead us to *repenting*, weeping, and seeking restoration from our personal, community, and institutional failures in the past and also in the present. These events of celebration and repentance can become powerful testimonies in those of us who *recognize our constant participation* in the circles of discernment. These events are, in addition, an expression of our continual need to adjust and align our (personal, community, and institutional) actions with the values of the kingdom of God. Therefore, we could see the need and might decide to include in our celebrations an "Institutional Day of Repentance, Confession, and Restoration." As heirs of the Reformation, in the context of this "celebration" we could arrive at the place of celebrating the successes as well as repenting of the failures in our discernment circles.[16] What a beautiful witness of reconciliation and restoration it would be to create a "Worship Service of Repentance." In this ceremony, each person, from the oldest to the youngest, could come forward, one by one, and lay upon the ground our "stones" of accusation, pain, bitterness, hate, and shame.[17] As an example of dialogue and forgiveness between church communities, we can mention the document "Healing Memories, Reconciling in Christ: Report of the Lutheran-Mennonite International Study Commission."

---

16. Here I have in mind the practice and festival of the Jewish people's Yom Kippur or Day of Repentance and Forgiveness.

17. I am using, somewhat freely, the scene found in John 8:2–11 in which Jesus invites us to forgiveness and reconciliation.

The Discernment Community as a Paradigm for a Continuing Reformation

In summary, we can celebrate the Reformation in our faith communities by creating and encouraging spaces for discernment guided by the Spirit. In these communities we need to maintain a clear awareness to the role and importance of these discernment spaces and how these spaces have influenced the life and practice of these communities. Therefore, we should promote communities that receive and offer forgiveness and restoration. In addition, we will avoid alliances and strategies that go against the essence of the gospel. This is possible because the members of these communities preserve the living memory and the evaluation of traditions by seeking to be guided in their life and ministry by the Spirit. This leads us to a final point.

Faithful Attempts

Third, in the process of celebrating and commemorating the Reformation, it is essential to see and evaluate the historical and theological emphases as faithful attempts of our discernment communities. Under the previous point, we emphasized the dynamic relationship between questions and responses, where we see the central role of these discernment communities. In this section, we want to emphasize the importance of how we perceive and use our shared beliefs or "confessions of faith" of a church or denomination.

Our Reflections and Practices as "Faithful Attempts"

In the context of our discernment communities or in those spaces where we make decisions, the form in which we perceive and the importance we give to the *nature* of our shared convictions (and those of others) is crucial. Traditionally, faced with alternative voices, we have tended to discredit, criticize, or attack "other" community and theological emphases. This has happened because we have assumed and placed the nature of our shared convictions as certainties that cannot be questioned. By holding this understanding of shared convictions, a person will tend to create, prioritize, and preserve spaces for discernment guided by the denial by us of the legitimate existence of others. For example, in our institutional spaces as professors, this denial might be expressed by the devaluing or mockery of alternative positions taken by colleagues, students, or theologians from other theological traditions. I am not suggesting that we blindly accept any and all theological or ethical positions, but rather I am suggesting that we develop "intellectual virtues" in our circles of discernment. This means we need to acknowledge that our beliefs and practices (and those of others) are faithful attempts to know and follow Jesus in our daily life.

Our "faithful attempts" to know and follow Jesus take place in and through our discernment circles and through the different activities of a local congregation. The idea of "faithful attempts" in our theological responses is trying to communicate the *trustworthy character of our search* in and through the Scriptures, the guidance of the Spirit, and our denominational tradition. In a similar way, it indicates the *transitory or in-process character* of creating our theological responses.

This vision of "faithful attempts" will become crucial in our spaces for dialogue and in the presence of voices that are different from ours. As we recognize our beliefs and practices as "faithful attempts," we can help ourselves by creating "spaces" for fellowship and discernment guided by love and grace. We can evaluate and respect our inherited theological emphases (and those of others) because we see them as the result of discernment circles in and through which our spiritual ancestors have discerned, prioritized, and preserved some of our denominational emphases. Following this point of view, we are acknowledging the work of God in and through our discernment circles and, at the same time, in and through other Christian denominations. The idea of "faithful attempts" suggests that just like our "spiritual ancestors," through our discernment circles we should participate in the process of carefully listening to each other, seeking the guidance of the Spirit, and responding to the specific challenges and situations of our contexts. Therefore, we are invited to create discernment circles in and through which we can discern, share, and learn from each other as we become communities of grace and reconciliation. As heirs of the Reformation, we can appreciate the faithfulness of our spiritual ancestors in their search to respond, in the light of the Bible and guided by the Spirit, to the vital questions of their own time and place. The invitation is for us to join with this "crowd of witnesses" in words and deeds, by creating discernment spaces by the Spirit. This will be possible to the degree that we look at our communities with a spirit of periphery and work so that our structures are at the service of God's kingdom.

Structures at the Service of God's Kingdom

To the degree that we value and become aware of our faithful attempts (fleshed out and expressed in our theological emphases and those of the "institutional culture"), it will be crucial to define and place our faithful attempts within the concept of *ministry*. The nature of our institutions, just like any of our ministries as the people of God, is such that their roots and their intentionality are shaped and based on the ministry of God.[18] The ministry of God is expressed by its search to reconcile the entire world with him.[19] The "faithful attempts" of our theological emphases and those of our institutional culture need to be occasionally reevaluated to see if they continue in symphony with the principles of the kingdom of God and the particular needs of our context.

The distinctions made by Kraybill regarding the kingdom, the church, and structures are appropriate here.[20] First, the kingdom of God has already begun, according to the gospels, with and through the life, ministry, death, and resurrection of Jesus. This kingdom is active in and through the Holy Spirit in our lives and relationships. Second, the *church* is the assembly of those who have accepted and welcomed the lordship of God in their lives and relationships.[21] As the church, we are members of a visible community that lives according to the principles of the kingdom. Finally, the *structures* are the "social vehicles," such as institutions and programs that exist to meet our own needs and those of others. The church structures (denominations, liturgy, mission agencies, etc.) should reflect the principles of the kingdom, but it is important to remember that these structures are not "the kingdom nor the church itself." Therefore, "we should periodically review these structures, human creations, to guarantee that they continue to be structures of service."[22] As a result, it is crucial to remember and identify our role and work as members of a community of faith within the framework of the work in God's kingdom.

In the process of seeking to be faithful to God in our specific contexts, we will necessarily propose and introduce adjustments to our community walk with God while we seek to hear and be obedient to the guidance of the Holy Spirit in our daily lives. These adjustments speak of our "faithful attempts" in the process of naming and identifying our relationships with God, among ourselves and with the rest of creation. The notion of "faithful attempts" communicates the idea of a discernment community that seeks to see, hear, experience, and live their lives in deep relationship with God and with their social surroundings. In addition, this notion is related to the idea of the provisional or "playful" nature of our "faithful attempts."[23] As a consequence, if we see our institutions and organizations as structures of service or as

---

18. See Barth, "Place of Theology."
19. R. Anderson, "A Theology for Ministry," in *Theological Foundations for Ministry*, 6–21.
20. Donald B. Kraybill, *The Upside-Down Kingdom* (Scottsdale: Herald, 1978), 171–78.
21. Kraybill, *Upside-Down Kingdom*, 173.
22. Kraybill, 173.
23. Rubem Alves, *La teología como juego* (Buenos Aires: La Aurora, 1982).

expressions of our "faithful attempts," we will be more inclined to enter into the process of evaluating and working toward the necessary adjustments. In summary, we can celebrate the spirit of the Reformation movement by valuing our structures as faithful attempts and not "sanctifying them." In addition, within the context of our communities and under the guidance of the Spirit, we will work so that they become *structures of service*, and *enable us to become agents* of God's kingdom. The distinctions of these concepts are a helpful reminder and motivation to see our models and alternatives of walking together in fellowship as "structures." As we evaluate our models of walking together, we will do so in light of and respect for the "past" (the person of Jesus, the prophets, apostles, church fathers, etc.) and with a view toward the "present" and the "future" as we trust in the continuing work of the Spirit.[24] As communities, we will evaluate if the current models and the "culture" of our structures are promoting service toward others and building up the community of faith in our specific contexts based on the values of God's kingdom.

Conclusion

I have proposed taking the community of discernment as the paradigmatic element and space for a continuing reformation. Our faith communities can offer and create *safe spaces* for the reflection and discernment of the various dimensions of knowing and following Jesus. In and through these discernment spaces we can confidently evaluate with gratitude the "faithful attempts" of our spiritual brothers and sisters from the past and transform them in communities of grace and reconciliation. We can also appreciate the "faithful attempts" of our faith communities or institutions in the present in our various attempts to manifest and communicate the grace and reconciliation of our God. In the process of these evaluations we can learn from each other about the multifaceted grace of God that is expressed in and through our faith communities, our theological traditions, and through all of creation.

I am proposing that we see and honor our discernment circles as essential elements because they *testify* to our continuing participation as disciples in our faith communities. These discernment circles represent the processes and actors/sectors that intervene in our "faithful attempts" to syntonize/synchronize our knowing and following Jesus as we listen to each other, read and interpret the Scriptures, and seek the guidance of the Spirit. It is

---

24. Stephen R. Holmes, *Listening to the Past: The Place of Tradition in Theology* (Carlisle: Paternoster, 2002), 1964.

foundational that in these circles we maintain the elements and members in dynamic tension and conversation. This permanent tension and conversation between the factors and members of the discernment circle is to seek to honor the discernment processes. In this way we will avoid giving undue privilege to one or a few powerful voices, or propose simplistic answers or absolute responses that are valid for all people in all places at all times. It will reduce the possibilities of providing, prioritizing, and preserving discernment spaces dominated by coercion and manipulation. On the contrary, if we honor these discernment circles, we can create *safe spaces* in and through which we can find support, mutual correction, and balance. This will happen only if we don't try to determine from the very beginning the result, the process, and the "players" in the discernment circles. We can create and find creative forms in which the various people and their voices can be honored. The invitation is to demonstrate an attitude that cares for the types of discernment circles that we are promoting, prioritizing, and preserving in our institutions, conferences, and agencies. The invitation is to see our discernment circles as those spaces in and through which we know and follow Jesus as members of our faith communities.

Therefore, as members of a faith community or denomination, we can confidently offer and share with "others" how our emphases (in my particular case, the Anabaptist tradition) of knowing and following Jesus can offer aspects and "flavors" to the Christian round table to the degree that we name and celebrate the grace and work of God in and through our communities. As heirs of the Reformation, we are invited to create and promote attitudes of vulnerability and interdependence as followers of Jesus as we seek and are open to be guided by the Spirit in light of our rich biblical, historical, and theological tradition. By honoring these discernment circles we are acknowledging the need to trust in others and the value (and diversity) of the gifts of each member who participates in the discernment process. As disciples we are acknowledging the permanent presence and work of the Holy Spirit in and through our discernment circles. In addition, we are recognizing and assuming our personal and community responsibility in discerning "appropriate" ways to know and follow Jesus in our community walk with God and in the process of transforming ourselves into communities of grace and reconciliation. In this way we can become a community that serves God's kingdom, and we can affirm that *ecclesia reformata, semper reformanda secundum verbum Dei* and through our discernment communities.

References

Alves, Rubem. "Las ideas teológicas y sus caminos por los surcos institucionales del protestantismo brasileño." In *Materiales para una teología en América Latina*, edited by Pablo Richard, 343–66. San José: DEI, 1980.

———. *La teología como juego*. Buenos Aires: La Aurora, 1982.

Anderson, R. "A Theology for Ministry." In *Theological Foundations for Ministry*, 6–21. Edinburgh: T&T Clark, 1979.

Banks, Robert J. *Paul's Idea of Community: The Early House Churches in Their Cultural Setting*. Peabody: Hendrickson, 1994.

Barth, Karl. "The Place of Theology." In *Theological Foundations for Ministry*, edited by R. Anderson, 22–58. Edinburgh: T&T Clark, 1979.

Driver, Juan. *La fe en la periferia de la historia: Una historia del pueblo cristiano desde la perspectiva de los movimientos de restauración y reforma radical*. Guatemala: CLARA-Semilla, 1997.

Dussel, Enrique. "Hipótesis para una historia de la teología en América Latina (1492–1980)." In *Materiales para una teología en América Latina*, edited by Pablo Richard, 401–52. San José: DEI, 1980.

Dyrness, William. *Temas de la teología del Antiguo Testamento*. Miami: Vida, 1989.

Gibellini, R. *La teología del siglo XX*. Santander: SAL TERRAE, 1998.

Holmes, Stephen R. *Listening to the Past: The Place of Tradition in Theology*. Carlisle: Paternoster, 2002.

Kraybill, Donald B. *The Upside-Down Kingdom*. Scottsdale: Herald, 1978.

Lowfink, Gerhard. *Jesus and Community: The Social Dimension of Christian Faith*. Philadelphia: Fortress, 1984.

Nordstokke, K. "La iglesia y el espacio político: una interpretación luterana." In *Libres por la gracia de Dios*, edited by A. Burghardt, 27–40. Geneva: La Federación Luterana Mundial, 2016.

Pope Francis. *Evangelii Gaudium*. Asuncion: Paulinas, HSP, 2013.

———. *Misericordia vultus: Bula de convocación del jubileo extraordinario de misericordia*. Asuncion: Paulinas HSP, 2016.

Roth, John D. *Teaching That Transforms: Why Anabaptist-Mennonite Education Matters*. Scottsdale: Herald, 2011.

Salinas, Daniel. *Taking up the Mantle: Latin American Evangelical Theology in the 20th Century*. Carlisle: Langham Global Library, 2017.

Sobrino, Jon. *Christ the Liberator: A View from the Victims*. Maryknoll: Orbis, 2001.

Suderman, Jack. *Re-Imagining the Church: Implications of Being a People in the World*. Eugene: Wipf and Stock, 2016.

Zaracho, Rafael. "The Role of Preferences in the Context of Believing and Discerning Communities: A Maturanian Reading." PhD diss., University of St. Andrews, 2014.

Langham Literature and its imprints are a ministry of Langham Partnership.

Langham Partnership is a global fellowship working in pursuit of the vision God entrusted to its founder John Stott –

> *to facilitate the growth of the church in maturity and Christ-likeness through raising the standards of biblical preaching and teaching.*

Our vision is to see churches in the Majority World equipped for mission and growing to maturity in Christ through the ministry of pastors and leaders who believe, teach and live by the word of God.

Our mission is to strengthen the ministry of the word of God through:
- nurturing national movements for biblical preaching
- fostering the creation and distribution of evangelical literature
- enhancing evangelical theological education

especially in countries where churches are under-resourced.

Our ministry

Langham Preaching partners with national leaders to nurture indigenous biblical preaching movements for pastors and lay preachers all around the world. With the support of a team of trainers from many countries, a multi-level programme of seminars provides practical training, and is followed by a programme for training local facilitators. Local preachers' groups and national and regional networks ensure continuity and ongoing development, seeking to build vigorous movements committed to Bible exposition.

Langham Literature provides Majority World preachers, scholars and seminary libraries with evangelical books and electronic resources through publishing and distribution, grants and discounts. The programme also fosters the creation of indigenous evangelical books in many languages, through writer's grants, strengthening local evangelical publishing houses, and investment in major regional literature projects, such as one volume Bible commentaries like *The Africa Bible Commentary* and *The South Asia Bible Commentary*.

Langham Scholars provides financial support for evangelical doctoral students from the Majority World so that, when they return home, they may train pastors and other Christian leaders with sound, biblical and theological teaching. This programme equips those who equip others. Langham Scholars also works in partnership with Majority World seminaries in strengthening evangelical theological education. A growing number of Langham Scholars study in high quality doctoral programmes in the Majority World itself. As well as teaching the next generation of pastors, graduated Langham Scholars exercise significant influence through their writing and leadership.

To learn more about Langham Partnership and the work we do visit **langham.org**

www.ingramcontent.com/pod-product-compliance
Lightning Source LLC
Chambersburg PA
CBHW050820160426
43192CB00010B/1838